SUPER EASY MEDITERRANEAN AIR FRYER COOKBOOK FOR BEGINNERS

Olivia Grace Thompson

Table of Contents

INTRODUCTION

The Mediterranean diet, celebrated for its holistic approach to health and delicious flavors, is a culinary journey through the bountiful landscapes surrounding the Mediterranean Sea.

In tandem with the Mediterranean diet's principles comes the innovative culinary tool – the air fryer. A compact kitchen companion, the air fryer harnesses the power of hot air circulation to achieve crispy and delightful textures without the need for excessive oil. It aligns seamlessly with the Mediterranean philosophy, offering a healthier way to prepare dishes while preserving the integrity of the vibrant flavors intrinsic to this beloved cuisine.

The Mediterranean Cuisine Combined with Air Fryer

Mediterranean cooking is not just a culinary style; it's a lifestyle that encapsulates health, simplicity, and a burst of rich flavors. Rooted in the traditional diets of countries bordering the Mediterranean Sea, this cuisine has become a global favorite, celebrated for its numerous benefits.

Health Benefits

One of the key pillars of Mediterranean cooking is its emphasis on fresh, wholesome components. The diet is rich in fruits, vegetables, whole grains, and olive oil - known for its heart-healthy properties. Fish, a lean source of protein, features prominently, contributing omega-3 fatty acids that support brain health and reduce the risk of chronic diseases. Adding herbs and spices like garlic and oregano to your meals not only makes them tastier but also brings health benefits. The Mediterranean diet, which includes these flavorful components, has been linked to a reduced chance of heart disease, diabetes, and some cancers. It's like a guide to eating well for a healthier life.

Time-Saving Aspects

Mediterranean cooking thrives on simplicity. The focus is on letting the natural flavors shine, minimizing the need for complicated techniques. Quick marinades, simple grilling, and one-pot wonders characterize the preparation methods. With an emphasis on fresh produce, minimal processing is required, ensuring a time-efficient approach to cooking. This simplicity not only saves time in the kitchen but also allows for a more relaxed and enjoyable cooking experience.

Adaptability to Various Skill Levels

Whether you're a seasoned chef or a novice in the kitchen, Mediterranean cooking caters to all skill levels. The recipes often rely on basic cooking methods, and the emphasis is on the quality of components rather than complex techniques. Novices can easily master classic dishes like Greek salads or roasted vegetables, while experienced cooks can explore more intricate recipes like paella or stuffed grape leaves. This adaptability fosters a sense of culinary inclusivity, making Mediterranean cooking accessible to everyone.

Budget-Friendliness

Mediterranean cooking celebrates simplicity, and this simplicity extends to the grocery list. With an emphasis on seasonal, local produce and affordable staples like legumes and grains, it's a budget-friendly culinary approach. Olive oil, a staple in Mediterranean cuisine, though slightly pricier, is used judiciously, making it an investment in both health and flavor. The cost-effectiveness of this cuisine allows individuals to embrace a healthier lifestyle without breaking the bank.

Rich Flavors

Mediterranean cooking is special because it can turn simple components into amazing dishes full of taste. Olive oil, garlic, lemon, and lots of herbs make a delicious mix of flavors. When you use fresh veggies, tasty herbs, and good quality proteins, you get a meal that feels really good and stays in your memory. Every bite has a story of tradition, culture, and a passion for food.

Air Fryer Technology and Mediterranean Cooking

Pairing Mediterranean recipes with air fryer technology is a match made in culinary heaven. Air fryers use hot air circulation to cook food, providing a healthier alternative to traditional frying methods. This aligns perfectly with the Mediterranean emphasis on health. The air fryer's efficiency is a time-saving boon, crisping up dishes without compromising the natural goodness of the components.

The adaptability of the air fryer to various skill levels complements the inclusivity of Mediterranean cooking. From simple vegetable roasts to more complex dishes like crispy falafel or fish fillets, the air fryer offers a hassle-free cooking experience for all.

Budget-friendly and eco-friendly, the air fryer consumes less oil, aligning with the Mediterranean approach to moderation. The technology enhances the natural flavors of components, ensuring that every bite is a celebration of health and taste.

Guide to Using an Air Fryer

Air fryers have emerged as versatile and efficient appliances, revolutionizing the way we approach cooking. These compact devices harness the power of hot air circulation to produce crispy and delicious results without the need for excessive oil. Whether you're a seasoned chef or a kitchen novice, understanding the fundamentals of air fryers can elevate your culinary journey, especially when delving into the world of Mediterranean cooking.

How Air Fryers Work

At the heart of an air fryer's magic is its ability to replicate the crispiness achieved through deep frying while significantly reducing the amount of oil used. The appliance features a heating element and a fan, working together to circulate hot air rapidly around the food. This high-speed air creates a crispy layer on the outside of your dishes, while the inside remains moist and flavorful. It's like a miniature convection oven with the added bonus of achieving a satisfying crunch without submerging your components in oil.

Benefits of Air Fryers

- **Healthier Cooking:** Air fryers provide a healthier alternative to traditional frying methods. By using minimal or no oil, you can enjoy your favorite fried treats with significantly fewer calories and less saturated fat.

- **Time Efficiency:** Air fryers are time-efficient, reducing cooking times compared to conventional methods. The rapid hot air circulation ensures that your dishes are cooked evenly and quickly.

- **Versatility:** These nifty appliances aren't limited to frying. Air fryers can also grill, roast, bake, and even reheat leftovers. Their versatility makes them a valuable addition to any kitchen.

- **Easy Cleanup:** Say goodbye to the mess associated with deep frying. Air fryers are designed with easy-to-clean baskets and trays, often dishwasher safe, making cleanup a breeze.

Practical Tips for Efficient Air Frying in Mediterranean Cooking

1. **Warm up:** Warm up your air fryer before cooking, similar to preheating an oven. This helps the hot air spread evenly, making your dish cook better.

2. **Use a Light Coating of Oil:** Use a little bit of oil: Air fryers need less oil than regular frying, but putting a small amount on your food can make it extra crispy. Opt for heart-healthy oils like olive oil, a staple in Mediterranean cooking.

3. **Don't Overcrowd the Basket:** To achieve that coveted crispiness, ensure there's enough space for air to circulate around the food. Overcrowding the basket can lead to uneven cooking.

4. **Shake or Flip Midway:** For even cooking, shake the basket or flip your components halfway through the cooking time. This simple step promotes uniform browning.

5. **Experiment with Mediterranean Flavors:** The air fryer is a perfect companion for Mediterranean cuisine. Try air-frying falafel, crispy vegetable skewers, or even fish fillets seasoned with a blend of aromatic herbs. The air fryer's efficiency enhances the natural flavors of Mediterranean components.

I'm excited to offer you a special gift to kick off your journey into Mediterranean cooking with an air fryer: the "Air Fryer Starter Guide." All it takes is a quick scan of the QR code here, and you'll have access to a wealth of tips and tricks:

- **Understanding Your Air Fryer**: Find out how it uses hot air to make your favorite fried foods in a healthier way.
- **Health Advantages**: See how cutting down on oil by up to 80% fits with the Mediterranean approach to eating healthily.
- **Time-Saving Tricks**: Learn how to make meals quickly that are also cooked evenly, making everything more convenient for you.
- **Beyond Frying**: Discover that your air fryer can also grill, roast, bake, and reheat, giving you lots of cooking options.
- **Cleaning Made Easy**: Appreciate how simple it is to clean, with dishwasher-safe parts that mean no hassle after cooking.
- **Recipes and Guidance**: Try out some delicious Mediterranean recipes that are perfect for air frying, along with professional guidance to improve your cooking.

*This guide is my way of **thanking you** for starting this flavorful exploration.*

Whether you're just beginning in the kitchen or you're already quite skilled, the "Air Fryer Starter Guide" is filled with valuable information to support you as you delve into the wonderful world of air frying.

The Basics of the Mediterranean Diet

The Mediterranean diet isn't just a culinary trend; it's a lifestyle that has withstood the test of time, rooted in the rich tapestry of cultures surrounding the Mediterranean Sea. Originating from countries like Greece, Italy, and Spain, this diet isn't just about what you eat but how you approach food. At its core, the Mediterranean diet is a celebration of fresh, flavorful, and wholesome components that contribute to overall well-being.

Origins of the Mediterranean Diet

The roots of the Mediterranean diet can be traced back thousands of years, finding its foundation in the traditional dietary patterns of communities bordering the Mediterranean Sea. It's a reflection of the lifestyle of these regions, where people historically enjoyed a diet abundant in fruits, vegetables, whole grains, fish, and olive oil. This dietary pattern emerged not just from the availability of local produce but also from cultural practices and a profound connection to the land and sea.

Key Principles

- **Abundance of Fresh Produce:** At the heart of the Mediterranean diet is an abundance of fresh fruits and vegetables. These nutrient-packed staples provide essential vitamins, minerals, and antioxidants, contributing to overall health and vitality.

- **Whole Grains:** In Mediterranean cooking, foods like barley, quinoa, and farro are important. They have lots of fiber, which is good for your digestion and gives you long-lasting energy.

- **Healthy Fats:** Olive oil, a cornerstone of the Mediterranean diet, replaces saturated fats with heart-healthy monounsaturated fats. This not only adds a distinctive flavor to dishes but also supports cardiovascular health.

- **Lean Proteins:** Fish and poultry take center stage in the Mediterranean diet, offering lean protein sources. Fish, in particular, is rich in omega-3 fatty acids, known for their anti-inflammatory properties and cognitive benefits.

- **Moderate Dairy:** While dairy is included, it's consumed in moderation. Greek yogurt and cheese provide calcium and protein without excessive saturated fats.

- **Herbs and Spices:** Mediterranean cuisine relies on a symphony of herbs and spices like basil, oregano, and garlic, not just for flavor but also for their potential health benefits, including anti-inflammatory and antioxidant properties.

Health Benefits

- **Heart Health:** The Mediterranean diet has gained acclaim for its positive impact on heart health. The inclusion of olive oil, fish, and a focus on unsaturated fats helps lower cholesterol levels and reduces the risk of cardiovascular diseases.

- **Weight Management:** Emphasizing whole, nutrient-dense foods, the Mediterranean diet supports weight management. The fiber content in fruits, vegetables, and whole grains promotes satiety, preventing overeating.

- **Reduced Inflammation:** The anti-inflammatory properties of the Mediterranean diet are attributed to the abundance of omega-3 fatty acids, antioxidants from fruits and vegetables, and the use of herbs and spices.

- **Improved Cognitive Function:** The omega-3 fatty acids found in fish, combined with antioxidants from fruits and vegetables, contribute to improved cognitive function and a lower risk of age-related cognitive decline.
- **Balanced Nutrition:** The diet's focus on a variety of food groups ensures a well-rounded nutritional profile, providing essential vitamins and minerals necessary for overall health.

As we delve into the fundamentals of the Mediterranean Diet, it's my pleasure to extend to you another exclusive offering designed to enrich your culinary and lifestyle journey. Introducing the **"Mediterranean Diet Guide,"** a comprehensive bonus resource available through a QR code on this page. This guide is crafted to deepen your understanding and appreciation of the Mediterranean Diet, highlighting its rich origins, key principles, and the myriad health benefits it offers:

- **In-depth Exploration of Origins:** Trace the roots of the Mediterranean Diet back to the ancient shores where it began, understanding its cultural and historical significance.
- **Guidance on Key Principles:** Learn about the abundance of fresh produce, the role of whole grains, the importance of healthy fats like olive oil, and the diet's emphasis on lean proteins and moderate dairy.
- **Highlight on Health Benefits:** Discover the myriad health advantages, from heart health and weight management to reduced inflammation and improved cognitive function.
- **Practical Tips for Implementation:** Beyond the principles, this guide offers practical advice on incorporating the Mediterranean Diet into your daily life, making it an accessible and enjoyable lifestyle choice.

To unlock this treasure trove of information, simply scan the QR code provided on this page. The **"Mediterranean Diet Guide"** is your gateway to embracing a lifestyle celebrated for its nutritional richness and connection to wellness and vitality.

This bonus is a token of gratitude for joining me on this journey. By exploring the Mediterranean Diet through this guide, you're not just adopting a way of eating; you're embracing a lifestyle that harmonizes nutrition with the joy of living.

Your adventure into the heart of Mediterranean wellness starts now. Let this guide inspire you to weave these timeless principles into the fabric of your daily life, enriching your health and savoring the deep flavors and joys of Mediterranean eating.

Essential Ingredients for Mediterranean Cuisine

Mediterranean cuisine, a treasure trove of vibrant flavors and healthful delights, derives its essence from a handful of key components that form the backbone of this culinary tradition. As we embark on a journey through the heart of Mediterranean cooking, let's explore the crucial components that create the symphony of taste unique to this region.

1. **Olive Oil:** At the core of Mediterranean cooking is the golden elixir – olive oil. Rich in monounsaturated fats and antioxidants, it not only imparts a distinctive flavor but also boasts numerous health benefits. When selecting olive oil for your pantry, opt for extra virgin varieties as they retain the highest nutritional value. Look for oils labeled cold-pressed and from reputable producers to ensure quality.

2. **Fresh Fruits and Vegetables:** The Mediterranean diet thrives on the abundance of fresh produce. Tomatoes, peppers, eggplants, zucchini, and a variety of leafy greens contribute to the vibrant colors and nutrient density of Mediterranean dishes. Aim for seasonal, locally sourced options to capture the peak of flavor and nutritional content. These vegetables are not only delicious but also a perfect fit for air fryer cooking, providing a crisp texture with minimal oil.

3. **Whole Grains:** Whole grains are the sturdy foundation of Mediterranean meals. Quinoa, farro, bulgur, and brown rice bring a nutty richness and fiber to the table. When selecting grains for your pantry, opt for whole, unprocessed varieties to maximize nutritional benefits. These grains are versatile in air fryer cooking, offering a delightful crunch when incorporated into dishes like grain bowls or as a crispy topping for salads.

4. **Seafood:** The Mediterranean Sea plays a pivotal role in shaping the cuisine of the region. Fish and seafood, such as salmon, sardines, and shrimp, are prominent protein sources. Rich in omega-3 fatty acids, these components contribute to heart health and add a delightful oceanic note to your dishes. When sourcing seafood, prioritize sustainably caught options for both ethical and environmental reasons.

5. **Herbs and Spices:** Herbs and spices are the magic wands of Mediterranean flavor. Basil, oregano, thyme, rosemary, and garlic infuse dishes with aromatic complexity. Cultivate a small herb garden if possible, or opt for fresh, high-quality herbs from local markets. These aromatic wonders not only enhance the taste of your air-fried creations but also bring an array of health benefits, from anti-inflammatory properties to digestive aids.

Guidance for Building a Mediterranean Pantry for Air Fryer Cooking

1. **Quality Over Quantity:** Prioritize quality components over quantity. Invest in a premium extra virgin olive oil, fresh herbs, and high-quality grains for an authentic Mediterranean experience.

2. **Seasonal and Local:** Embrace the seasons and source components locally when possible. This not only ensures freshness but also supports local farmers and sustainable agriculture.

3. **Diversify Seafood Choices:** Explore a variety of seafood options to keep your meals exciting. Incorporate different fish and shellfish to capture the diverse flavors of the Mediterranean.

4. **Experiment with Herbs and Spices:** Don't be afraid to experiment with a variety of herbs and spices. Create your spice blends or explore Mediterranean blends for a convenient and authentic flavor profile.

5. **Mindful Air Frying:** Use the air fryer to your advantage by experimenting with different textures and flavors. Roast vegetables, air-fry whole grain pita chips, or crisp up seafood with minimal oil for a healthy and delicious outcome.

1. Greek-style Air Fryer Breakfast Potatoes

Preparation time: 10 minutes
Cooking time: 20 minutes
Servings: 4
Ingredients:

- 4 cups baby potatoes, divided
- 2 tbsps. olive oil
- 1 tsp. dried oregano
- 1 tsp. garlic powder
- Salt and pepper as required

Directions:

1. In your bowl, toss potatoes using olive oil, oregano, garlic powder, salt, and pepper.
2. Warm up the air fryer to 400 °F.
3. Air fry potatoes for 20 minutes or 'til golden brown and crispy.
4. Serve hot.

Per serving: Calories: 180kcal; Fat: 7g; Carbs: 28g; Protein: 3g

2. Mediterranean Breakfast Burritos with Hummus

Preparation time: 15 minutes
Cooking time: 10 minutes
Servings: 2
Ingredients:

- 4 big tortillas
- 1 cup hummus
- 1 cup diced cucumber
- 1 cup diced tomatoes
- 1/2 cup crumbled feta cheese
- Fresh parsley for garnish

Directions:

1. Warm up the air fryer to 400 °F.
2. Disperse a generous layer of your hummus onto each tortilla.
3. Layer with diced cucumber, diced tomatoes, and crumbled feta cheese.
4. Fold the sides of the tortilla in and roll tightly to form a burrito.
5. Put burritos in to your air fryer basket.
6. Air fry for 10 minutes or 'til the burritos are golden and crispy.
7. Garnish with fresh parsley prior to presenting.

Per serving: Calories: 480kcal; Fat: 25g; Carbs: 47g; Protein: 16g

3. Tomato and Olive Breakfast Flatbreads

Preparation time: 10 minutes
Cooking time: 10 minutes
Servings: 2
Ingredients:

- 2 whole wheat flatbreads
- 1 cup cherry tomatoes, divided
- 1/4 cup cut black olives
- 1/2 cup crumbled feta cheese
- 2 tbsps. chopped fresh basil
- Olive oil spray
- Salt and pepper as required

Directions:

1. Warm up the air fryer to 375 °F.
2. Put flatbreads in to your air fryer basket.
3. Spray the flatbreads using olive oil and sprinkle with salt and pepper.
4. Top with cherry tomatoes, cut black olives, and crumbled feta.
5. Air fry for 10 minutes or 'til the flatbreads are crispy and the toppings are heated.
6. Sprinkle with chopped fresh basil prior to presenting.

Per serving: Calories: 320kcal; Fat: 15g; Carbs: 36g; Protein: 12g

4. Air-Fried Olive and Herb Breadsticks

Preparation time: 15 minutes
Cooking time: 10 minutes
Servings: 4
Ingredients:

- 1 package refrigerated pizza dough
- 1/4 cup black olives, chopped
- 1 tbsp. fresh rosemary, chopped
- 2 tbsps. olive oil
- 1/2 tsp. garlic powder
- Salt as required

Directions:

1. Warm up the air fryer to 375 °F.
2. Roll out the pizza dough and cut into strips.
3. In your bowl, mix olives, rosemary, olive oil, garlic powder, and salt.
4. Brush each strip with the olive mixture and twist.
5. Air fry for 10 minutes or 'til golden brown.
6. Serve warm.

Per serving: Calories: 220kcal; Fat: 10g; Carbs: 28g; Protein: 5g

5. Lemon and Herb Ricotta Stuffed Mushrooms

Preparation time: 10 minutes
Cooking time: 15 minutes
Servings: 3
Ingredients:

- 12 big mushrooms, stems taken out and finely chopped
- 1 cup ricotta cheese
- Zest of 1 lemon
- 2 tbsps. chopped fresh herbs (e.g., parsley or thyme)
- 2 pieces garlic, crushed
- Salt and pepper as required
- Olive oil spray

Directions:

1. Warm up the air fryer to 375 °F.
2. In your bowl, mix together chopped mushroom stems, ricotta cheese, lemon zest, chopped herbs, crushed garlic, salt, and pepper.
3. Stuff each mushroom cap with the ricotta mixture.
4. Mildly spray the air fryer basket using olive oil.
5. Place stuffed mushrooms in the basket.
6. Air fry for 15 minutes or 'til the mushrooms are tender and the ricotta is golden.

Per serving: Calories: 180kcal; Fat: 12g; Carbs: 8g; Protein: 12g

6. Sundried Tomato and Olive Frittata Muffins

Preparation time: 10 minutes
Cooking time: 15 minutes
Servings: 4
Ingredients:

- 6 big eggs
- 1/4 cup milk
- 1/2 cup chopped sundried tomatoes (drained if packed in oil)
- 1/4 cup cut black olives
- 1/4 cup crumbled feta cheese
- Salt and pepper as required
- Cooking spray

Directions:

1. Warm up the air fryer to 350 °F.
2. In your bowl, whisk together eggs, milk, salt, sundried tomatoes, black olives, feta cheese, and pepper.
3. Spray the muffin cups using cooking spray.
4. Pour egg mixture evenly into your muffin cups.
5. Place muffin cups in to your air fryer basket.
6. Air fry for 15 minutes or 'til the frittata muffins are set and slightly golden.
7. Prior to distributing, let them cool for a couple of minutes before they are served.

Per serving: Calories: 180kcal; Fat: 12g; Carbs: 5g; Protein: 13g

7. Air-Fried Shakshuka Bites

Preparation time: 10 minutes
Cooking time: 10 minutes
Servings: 4
Ingredients:

- 4 big eggs
- 1 cup marinara sauce
- 1/2 cup crumbled feta cheese
- 1 tsp. ground cumin
- 1/2 tsp. smoked paprika
- Salt and pepper as required

Directions:

1. Warm up the air fryer to 375 °F.
2. Split the marinara sauce among four wells in an air fryer-friendly pan.
3. Make a well in the sauce and crack an egg into each well.
4. Sprinkle feta cheese, cumin, smoked paprika, salt, and pepper over the top.
5. Fry the eggs in an air fryer for 10 minutes, or until they reach the desired level of doneness.

Per serving: Calories: 230kcal; Fat: 15g; Carbs: 11g; Protein: 13g

8. Mediterranean Veggie Omelet

Preparation time: 10 minutes
Cooking time: 8 minutes
Servings: 2
Ingredients:

- 4 big eggs
- 1/4 cup diced bell peppers
- 1/4 cup diced tomatoes
- 2 tbsps. chopped red onions
- 2 tbsps. crumbled feta cheese
- Salt and pepper as required

Directions:

1. In your bowl, whisk together eggs, bell peppers, tomatoes, red onions, feta cheese, salt, and pepper.
2. Pour mixture into the air fryer basket.
3. Warm up the air fryer to 350 °F then cook for 8 minutes or 'til the omelet is cooked through.
4. Carefully remove the omelet, slice, and serve.

Per serving: Calories: 220kcal; Fat: 15g; Carbs: 5g; Protein: 16g

9. Roasted Red Pepper and Feta Egg Cups

Preparation time: 10 minutes
Cooking time: 12 minutes
Servings: 4
Ingredients:

- 4 big eggs
- 1/4 cup roasted red peppers, chopped
- 1/4 cup feta cheese, crumbled
- 1 tbsp. fresh chives, chopped
- Salt and pepper as required

Directions:

1. Warm up the air fryer to 350 °F.
2. Grease four ramekins and crack an egg into each.
3. Top with roasted red peppers, feta cheese, chives, salt, and pepper.
4. Air fry for 12 minutes or 'til the eggs are set to your liking.
5. Serve warm.

Per serving: Calories: 150kcal; Fat: 10g; Carbs: 4g; Protein: 11g

10. Air Fryer Greek Omelet Roll-Ups

Preparation time: 10 minutes
Cooking time: 8 minutes
Servings: 2
Ingredients:

- 4 big eggs
- 1/4 cup diced tomatoes
- 1/4 cup cut black olives
- 2 tbsps. crumbled feta cheese
- 1 tbsp. fresh oregano, chopped
- Salt and pepper as required

Directions:

1. In your bowl, whisk together eggs, tomatoes, black olives, feta cheese, oregano, salt, and pepper.
2. Pour mixture into the air fryer basket.
3. Warm up the air fryer to 350 °F then cook for 8 minutes or 'til the omelet is cooked through.
4. Carefully remove the omelet, slice, and roll into individual servings.
5. Serve warm.

Per serving: Calories: 220kcal; Fat: 15g; Carbs: 5g; Protein: 16g

11. Herbed Feta and Tomato Breakfast Quesadillas

Preparation time: 10 minutes
Cooking time: 10 minutes
Servings: 2
Ingredients:

- 4 small flour tortillas
- 1 cup crumbled feta cheese
- 1 cup diced tomatoes
- 2 tbsps. chopped fresh herbs (e.g., basil or oregano)
- Salt and pepper as required
- Cooking spray

Directions:

1. Warm up the air fryer to 375 °F.
2. In your bowl, mix together crumbled feta, diced tomatoes, chopped herbs, salt, and pepper.
3. Put a portion of the feta mixture on one half of each tortilla.
4. Fold the tortillas in half to create a semi-circle.
5. Mildly spray the air fryer basket using cooking spray.
6. Arrange the quesadillas in the basket.
7. Air fry for 10 minutes or 'til the tortillas are crispy and the filling is heated through.

Per serving: Calories: 320kcal; Fat: 18g; Carbs: 32g; Protein: 12g

12. Spinach and Feta Breakfast Wraps

Preparation time: 15 minutes
Cooking time: 10 minutes
Servings: 2
Ingredients:

- 4 big whole wheat tortillas
- 2 cups fresh spinach leaves
- 1 cup crumbled feta cheese
- 1 cup diced tomatoes
- 4 big eggs
- Salt and pepper as required
- Cooking spray

Directions:

1. Warm up the air fryer to 375 °F.
2. In your pan, sauté spinach 'til wilted.
3. In your bowl, whisk together eggs, salt, and pepper.
4. Scramble the eggs in the same pan with the wilted spinach 'til cooked.
5. Lay out the tortillas then divide the scrambled eggs evenly among them.
6. Top each with crumbled feta and diced tomatoes.
7. Roll the tortillas tightly to form wraps.
8. Mildly spray the air fryer basket using cooking spray.
9. Put wraps in the basket.
10. Air fry for 10 minutes or 'til the wraps are heated through and slightly crispy.

Per serving: Calories: 420kcal; Fat: 22g; Carbs: 36g; Protein: 20g

13. Greek-style Air Fryer Bagel with Cream Cheese

Preparation time: 5 minutes
Cooking time: 3 minutes
Servings: 2
Ingredients:

- 2 whole-grain bagels, divided
- 1/2 cup Greek cream cheese
- 1/4 cup cherry tomatoes, cut
- 1/4 cup cucumber, cut
- 2 tbsps. Kalamata olives, chopped
- Fresh dill for garnish

Directions:

1. Warm up the air fryer to 350 °F.
2. Air fry bagel halves for 3 minutes or 'til toasted.
3. Disperse Greek cream cheese on each bagel half.
4. Top with cut cherry tomatoes, cucumber, and chopped Kalamata olives.
5. Garnish with fresh dill and serve.

Per serving: Calories: 280kcal; Fat: 12g; Carbs: 36g; Protein: 8g

14. Air Fryer Eggplant Bruschetta

Preparation time: 15 minutes
Cooking time: 15 minutes
Servings: 4
Ingredients:

- 1 big eggplant, cut into 1/2-inch rounds
- Olive oil spray
- 1 cup diced tomatoes
- 1/4 cup chopped fresh basil
- 2 pieces garlic, crushed
- 2 tbsps. balsamic vinegar
- Salt and pepper as required
- 1/2 cup shredded mozzarella cheese
- Balsamic glaze for drizzling (optional)

Directions:

1. Warm up the air fryer to 375 °F.
2. Spray eggplant slices with olive oil on both sides.
3. Place eggplant slices in your air fryer basket in a single layer.
4. Air fry for a total of 10 minutes, flipping halfway through, or until the eggplant is golden and tender.
5. In a bowl, mix diced tomatoes, chopped basil, crushed garlic, balsamic vinegar, salt, and pepper.
6. Top each air-fried eggplant slice with the tomato mixture.
7. Sprinkle shredded mozzarella on top.
8. Return the topped eggplant slices to the air fryer for an extra 5 minutes or 'til the cheese is melted and bubbly.
9. Drizzle using balsamic glaze if desired prior to presenting.

Per serving: Calories: 120kcal; Fat: 5g; Carbs: 16g; Protein: 5g

15. Tomato and Olive Bruschetta Toast

Preparation time: 10 minutes
Cooking time: 5 minutes
Servings: 4
Ingredients:

- 4 slices of whole-grain bread
- 1 cup diced tomatoes
- 1/4 cup cut black olives
- 2 tbsps. chopped fresh basil
- 2 tbsps. extra-virgin olive oil
- 1 piece garlic, crushed
- Salt and pepper as required

Directions:

1. Warm up the air fryer to 375 °F.
2. In your bowl, mix together diced tomatoes, cut black olives, chopped fresh basil, crushed garlic, olive oil, salt, and pepper.
3. Place slices of bread in to your air fryer basket.
4. Spoon the tomato and olive mixture onto each slice of bread.
5. Air fry for 5 minutes or 'til the bread is toasted and the topping is heated.
6. Serve immediately.

Per serving: Calories: 180kcal; Fat: 9g; Carbs: 21g; Protein: 4g

16. Air-Fried Mediterranean Quiche Bites

Preparation time: 15 minutes
Cooking time: 12 minutes
Servings: 6
Ingredients:

- 4 big eggs
- 1/2 cup milk
- 1/2 cup crumbled feta cheese
- 1/4 cup black olives, chopped
- 1/4 cup sun-dried tomatoes, chopped
- 2 tbsps. fresh basil, chopped
- Salt and pepper as required

Directions:

1. Warm up the air fryer to 350 °F.
2. In your bowl, whisk together eggs, milk, feta cheese, black olives, sun-dried tomatoes, basil, salt, and pepper.
3. Grease a muffin tin then pour the egg mixture evenly into each cup.
4. Air fry for 12 minutes or 'til the quiche bites are set.
5. Serve warm.

Per serving: Calories: 120kcal; Fat: 8g; Carbs: 5g; Protein: 8g

17. Mediterranean Breakfast Pita Pockets

Preparation time: 15 minutes
Cooking time: 10 minutes
Servings: 2
Ingredients:

- 2 whole wheat pita pockets
- 4 big eggs
- 1 cup diced cucumber
- 1 cup diced bell peppers (assorted colors)
- 1/2 cup crumbled feta cheese
- 2 tbsps. chopped fresh parsley
- Salt and pepper as required

Directions:

1. Warm up the air fryer to 375 °F.
2. Cut each pita pocket in half to create pockets.
3. In your bowl, whisk together eggs, salt, and pepper.
4. Scramble the eggs in a pan 'til cooked.
5. Fill each pita pocket with scrambled eggs, diced cucumber, diced bell peppers, crumbled feta, and chopped parsley.
6. Place filled pita pockets in to your air fryer basket.
7. Air fry for 10 minutes or 'til the pockets are heated through.

Per serving: Calories: 380kcal; Fat: 18g; Carbs: 38g; Protein: 20g

18. Spinach and Feta Stuffed Breakfast Peppers

Preparation time: 15 minutes
Cooking time: 12 minutes
Servings: 4
Ingredients:

- 4 big bell peppers, divided and seeds taken out
- 2 cups baby spinach, chopped
- 1/2 cup crumbled feta cheese
- 4 big eggs
- 1 tsp. dried oregano
- Salt and pepper as required

Directions:

1. Warm up the air fryer to 375 °F.
2. In your bowl, mix chopped spinach, feta cheese, eggs, dried oregano, salt, and pepper.
3. Stuff each bell pepper half with the spinach and feta mixture.
4. Make sure the peppers are soft and the filling is set by air-frying them for a period of 12 minutes.
5. Serve warm.

Per serving: Calories: 180kcal; Fat: 11g; Carbs: 10g; Protein: 12g

19. Air Fryer Halloumi and Tomato Skewers

Preparation time: 10 minutes
Cooking time: 10 minutes
Servings: 2
Ingredients:

- 8 cherry tomatoes
- 8 slices of halloumi cheese
- 1 tbsp. olive oil
- 1 tsp. dried oregano
- Salt and pepper as required
- Wooden skewers

Directions:

1. Warm up the air fryer to 400 °F.
2. Thread cherry tomatoes and halloumi slices onto the skewers alternately.
3. In your small bowl, mix olive oil, dried oregano, salt, and pepper.
4. Brush skewers with the olive oil mixture.
5. Place skewers in to your air fryer basket.
6. Air fry for 10 minutes or 'til the halloumi is golden and tomatoes are tender.

Per serving: Calories: 280kcal; Fat: 23g; Carbs: 5g; Protein: 14g

20. Mediterranean Veggie Breakfast Skewers

Preparation time: 15 minutes
Cooking time: 8 minutes
Servings: 4
Ingredients:

- 1 zucchini, cut
- 1 cup cherry tomatoes
- 1/2 cup red onion, diced
- 1/2 cup bell peppers, diced
- 1/4 cup black olives
- 2 tbsps. olive oil
- 1 tsp. dried oregano
- Salt and pepper as required

Directions:

1. Warm up the air fryer to 375 °F.
2. Thread zucchini, cherry tomatoes, red onion, bell peppers, and olives onto skewers.
3. Brush using olive oil and sprinkle with dried oregano, salt, and pepper.
4. Air fry for 8 minutes or 'til veggies are tender.
5. Serve warm.

Per serving: Calories: 120kcal; Fat: 8g; Carbs: 10g; Protein: 2g

 # APPETIZER AND SNACKS

21. Greek Spanakopita Triangles

Preparation time: 20 minutes
Cooking time: 10 minutes
Servings: 4 (12 triangles)
Ingredients:

- 2 cups frozen chopped spinach
- 1 cup feta cheese, crumbled
- 1/2 cup ricotta cheese
- 1/4 cup grated Parmesan cheese
- 1/4 cup fresh dill, chopped
- 1/4 cup fresh parsley, chopped
- 1 piece garlic, crushed
- Salt and pepper as required
- 12 sheets phyllo dough, thawed
- Olive oil for brushing

Directions:

1. In your bowl, mix together spinach, feta cheese, ricotta cheese, Parmesan cheese, dill, parsley, garlic, salt, and pepper.
2. Cut phyllo dough into 4x4-inch squares.
3. Position a dollop of the spinach mixture in the middle of each square using a dessert spoon.
4. Fold the dough into triangles, brushing each using olive oil.
5. Warm up the air fryer to 375 °F.
6. Air fry the triangles for 10 minutes or 'til golden brown.
7. Serve warm.

Per serving: Calories: 320kcal; Fat: 18g; Carbs: 30g; Protein: 10g

22. Spinach and Artichoke Dip Stuffed Mushrooms

Preparation time: 15 minutes
Cooking time: 10 minutes
Servings: 4 (16 pieces)
Ingredients:

- 16 big mushrooms, cleaned and stems taken out
- 1 cup frozen chopped spinach
- 1/2 cup artichoke hearts, chopped
- 1/2 cup cream cheese, softened
- 1/4 cup mayonnaise
- 1/4 cup grated Parmesan cheese
- 1/4 cup shredded mozzarella cheese
- 1 piece garlic, crushed
- Salt and pepper as required

Directions:

1. Warm up the air fryer to 375 °F.
2. In your bowl, mix together spinach, artichoke hearts, cream cheese, mayonnaise, Parmesan cheese, mozzarella cheese, garlic, salt, and pepper.
3. Stuff each mushroom with the spinach and artichoke mixture.
4. Using an air fryer, cook the mushrooms for 10 minutes, or until they are soft and the filling is golden brown.
5. Serve warm.

Per serving: Calories: 180kcal; Fat: 15g; Carbs: 6g; Protein: 6g

23. Air-Fried Feta and Olive Puff Pastry Bites

Preparation time: 15 minutes
Cooking time: 10 minutes
Servings: 4 (16 bites)
Ingredients:

- 1 sheet puff pastry, thawed
- 1/2 cup feta cheese, crumbled
- 1/4 cup Kalamata olives, chopped
- 1 tbsp. fresh oregano, chopped
- Olive oil for brushing

Directions:

1. Warm up the air fryer to 375 °F.
2. Roll out the puff pastry and cut into 2-inch squares.
3. In your bowl, mix together feta cheese, olives, and oregano.
4. Put a small spoonful of the feta mixture in the middle of each square.
5. Fold the corners to form a bite-sized puff pastry.
6. Brush using olive oil and air fry for 10 minutes or 'til golden brown.
7. Serve warm.

Per serving: Calories: 240kcal; Fat: 18g; Carbs: 15g; Protein: 6g

24. Mediterranean Bruschetta with Tomato and Basil

Preparation time: 10 minutes
Cooking time: 5 minutes
Servings: 4
Ingredients:

- 1 baguette, cut
- 2 cups cherry tomatoes, diced
- 1/4 cup fresh basil, chopped
- 2 pieces garlic, crushed
- 3 tbsps. extra-virgin olive oil
- Balsamic glaze for drizzling
- Salt and pepper as required

Directions:

1. Warm up the air fryer to 375 °F.
2. Put baguette slices in to your air fryer and toast for 5 minutes or 'til golden.
3. In your bowl, combine diced tomatoes, basil, crushed garlic, olive oil, salt, and pepper.
4. Top each toasted baguette slice using the tomato and basil mixture.
5. Drizzle with balsamic glaze prior to presenting.

Per serving: Calories: 220kcal; Fat: 12g; Carbs: 24g; Protein: 4g

25. Air Fryer Falafel Bites with Tzatziki Sauce

Preparation time: 18 minutes
Cooking time: 12 minutes
Servings: 4 (16 bites)
Ingredients:

- 1 can (15 oz) chickpeas
- 1/2 cup fresh parsley, chopped
- 1/4 cup red onion, chopped
- 2 pieces garlic, crushed
- 1 tsp. ground cumin
- 1 tsp. ground coriander
- 1/2 tsp. baking powder
- Salt and pepper as required
- Olive oil for brushing
- Tzatziki sauce for dipping

Directions:

1. In the blending container that you have, blend chickpeas, parsley, red onion, garlic, cumin, coriander, baking powder, salt, and pepper 'til a coarse mixture forms.
2. Form the mixture into small falafel bites.
3. Warm up the air fryer to 375 °F.
4. Brush falafel bites using olive oil and air fry for 12 minutes or 'til golden brown then cooked through.
5. Serve with tzatziki sauce for dipping.

Per serving: Calories: 180kcal; Fat: 10g; Carbs: 18g; Protein: 6g

26. Air-Fried Stuffed Mushrooms with Sun-Dried Tomatoes

Preparation time: 15 minutes
Cooking time: 10 minutes
Servings: 4 (16 pieces)
Ingredients:

- 16 big mushrooms, cleaned and stems taken out
- 1/2 cup sun-dried tomatoes, chopped
- 1/4 cup feta cheese, crumbled
- 2 tbsps. fresh parsley, chopped
- 2 pieces garlic, crushed
- Olive oil for brushing
- Salt and pepper as required

Directions:

1. Warm up the air fryer to 375 °F.
2. In your bowl, mix sun-dried tomatoes, feta cheese, fresh parsley, crushed garlic, salt, and pepper.
3. Stuff each mushroom with the mixture.
4. Brush the mushrooms using olive oil.
5. Air fry for 10 minutes or 'til the mushrooms are tender.
6. Serve warm.

Per serving: Calories: 160kcal; Fat: 8g; Carbs: 18g; Protein: 6g

27. Lemon Garlic Marinated Olives

Preparation time: 10 minutes
Cooking time: 5 minutes
Servings: 4
Ingredients:

- 2 cups mixed olives
- 2 tbsps. olive oil
- Zest of 1 lemon
- 2 pieces garlic, crushed
- 1 tsp. dried oregano
- 1/2 tsp. red pepper flakes (optional)

Directions:

1. In your bowl, mix together lemon zest, garlic, oregano, olives, olive oil, and red pepper flakes.
2. Let the olives marinate for almost 1 hour.
3. Warm up the air fryer to 350 °F.
4. Air fry marinated olives for 5 minutes to warm them.
5. Serve at room temp.

Per serving: Calories: 180kcal; Fat: 18g; Carbs: 5g; Protein: 1g

28. Greek-style Spinach and Feta Phyllo Cups

Preparation time: 15 minutes
Cooking time: 10 minutes
Servings: 4 (12 cups)
Ingredients:

- 12 mini phyllo cups (store-bought)
- 1 cup frozen chopped spinach
- 1/2 cup feta cheese, crumbled
- 1/4 cup red onion, finely chopped
- 1/4 cup Kalamata olives, chopped
- 1 tbsp. fresh dill, chopped
- Olive oil for brushing

Directions:

1. Warm up the air fryer to 375 °F.
2. In your bowl, mix together spinach, feta cheese, red onion, Kalamata olives, and fresh dill.
3. Put a spoonful of the mixture into each phyllo cup.
4. Brush the tops using olive oil.
5. Air fry for 10 minutes or 'til the phyllo cups are golden brown.
6. Serve warm.

Per serving: Calories: 150kcal; Fat: 10g; Carbs: 12g; Protein: 4g

29. Hummus-Stuffed Mini Bell Peppers

Preparation time: 15 minutes
Cooking time: 8 minutes
Servings: 4 (16 pieces)
Ingredients:

- 16 mini bell peppers, divided and seeds taken out
- 1 cup hummus
- Cherry tomatoes for garnish
- Fresh parsley for garnish

Directions:

1. Warm up the air fryer to 375 °F.
2. Fill each mini bell pepper half with hummus.
3. Place stuffed peppers in to your air fryer basket.
4. Air fry for 8 minutes or 'til the peppers are tender.
5. Garnish with cherry tomatoes and fresh parsley prior to presenting.

Per serving: Calories: 120kcal; Fat: 6g; Carbs: 15g; Protein: 4g

30. Roasted Red Pepper and Walnut Dip

Preparation time: 10 minutes
Cooking time: 15 minutes
Servings: 4
Ingredients:

- 1 cup roasted red peppers, drained
- 1/2 cup walnuts, toasted
- 1/4 cup olive oil
- 2 tbsps. breadcrumbs
- 1 piece garlic, crushed
- 1 tsp. ground cumin
- Salt and pepper as required

Directions:

1. Warm up the air fryer to 375 °F.
2. In the blending container that you have, blend roasted red peppers, walnuts, olive oil, breadcrumbs, garlic, cumin, salt, and pepper 'til smooth.
3. Put the mixture in a dish that can be placed in the oven.
4. Air fry for 15 minutes or 'til the dip is heated through.
5. Serve with pita chips or veggies.

Per serving: Calories: 200kcal; Fat: 18g; Carbs: 8g; Protein: 3g

31. Feta-Stuffed Dates Wrapped in Prosciutto

Preparation time: 15 minutes
Cooking time: 5 minutes
Servings: 4 (16 pieces)
Ingredients:

- 16 Medjool dates, pitted
- 1/2 cup feta cheese, crumbled
- 8 slices prosciutto, divided lengthwise

Directions:

1. Warm up the air fryer to 375 °F.
2. Stuff each date with a tsp. of feta cheese.
3. Fold a half slice of prosciutto over each of the dates and set them aside.
4. Place wrapped dates in to your air fryer basket.
5. Air fry for 5 minutes or 'til the prosciutto is crispy.
6. Serve warm.

Per serving: Calories: 180kcal; Fat: 8g; Carbs: 25g; Protein: 5g

32. Air-Fried Halloumi Fries with Marinara Dipping Sauce

Preparation time: 15 minutes
Cooking time: 10 minutes
Servings: 4
Ingredients:

- 1 block halloumi cheese, cut into fries
- 1/2 cup breadcrumbs
- 1/4 cup grated Parmesan cheese
- 1 tsp. smoked paprika
- Marinara sauce for dipping

Directions:

1. Warm up the air fryer to 375 °F.
2. In your bowl, mix breadcrumbs, grated Parmesan, and smoked paprika.
3. Coat halloumi fries in the breadcrumb mixture.
4. Arrange halloumi fries in to your air fryer basket.
5. Air fry for 10 minutes or 'til golden and crispy.
6. Serve with marinara sauce for dipping.

Per serving: Calories: 280kcal; Fat: 18g; Carbs: 15g; Protein: 16g

33. Olive and Herb Pita Chips

Preparation time: 10 minutes
Cooking time: 5 minutes
Servings: 4
Ingredients:

- 4 whole-wheat pita bread
- 1/4 cup olive oil
- 1/4 cup mixed olives, chopped
- 1 tbsp. fresh rosemary, chopped
- Salt and pepper as required

Directions:

1. Warm up the air fryer to 375 °F.
2. Brush each pita bread using olive oil and sprinkle with chopped olives and rosemary.
3. Cut pita bread into wedges.
4. Air fry for 5 minutes or 'til the pita chips are crispy.
5. Season using salt and pepper.

Per serving: Calories: 220kcal; Fat: 14g; Carbs: 20g; Protein: 4g

34. Zucchini and Feta Fritters

Preparation time: 18 minutes
Cooking time: 12 minutes
Servings: 4 (12 fritters)
Ingredients:

- 2 medium zucchinis, grated and drained
- 1/2 cup feta cheese, crumbled
- 1/4 cup fresh parsley, chopped
- 1/4 cup breadcrumbs
- 1/4 cup grated Parmesan cheese
- 2 eggs, beaten
- 1 piece garlic, crushed
- Salt and pepper as required
- Olive oil spray

Directions:

1. In your bowl, mix together grated zucchini, feta cheese, parsley, breadcrumbs, Parmesan cheese, eggs, crushed garlic, salt, and pepper.
2. Form the mixture into small fritters.
3. Warm up the air fryer to 375 °F.
4. Spray the fritters using olive oil and air fry for 12 minutes or 'til golden brown.
5. Serve warm with tzatziki sauce.

Per serving: Calories: 180kcal; Fat: 10g; Carbs: 14g; Protein: 9g

35. Crispy Za'atar Chickpeas

Preparation time: 5 minutes
Cooking time: 15 minutes
Servings: 4
Ingredients:

- 2 cans (15 oz each) chickpeas
- 2 tbsps. olive oil
- 2 tbsps. za'atar spice blend
- 1 tsp. garlic powder
- Salt as required

Directions:

1. In your bowl, toss chickpeas using olive oil, za'atar, garlic powder, and salt.
2. Warm up the air fryer to 375 °F.
3. Air fry chickpeas for 15 minutes, shaking the basket every 5 minutes for even cooking.
4. Let them cool prior to presenting.

Per serving: Calories: 220kcal; Fat: 10g; Carbs: 28g; Protein: 9g

36. Mediterranean Stuffed Grape Leaves (Dolma)

Preparation time: 15 minutes
Cooking time: 15 minutes
Servings: 4 (16 pieces)
Ingredients:

- 1 cup grape leaves, preserved in brine, drained
- 1 cup cooked rice
- 1/2 cup pine nuts, toasted
- 1/4 cup fresh dill, chopped
- 1/4 cup fresh mint, chopped
- 1/4 cup lemon juice
- 2 tbsps. olive oil
- Salt and pepper as required

Directions:

1. In your bowl, mix together cooked rice, pine nuts, dill, mint, lemon juice, olive oil, salt, and pepper.
2. Put a grape leaf flat on a surface then add a spoonful of the rice mixture in the middle.
3. Fold the sides and roll to form a tight cylinder.
4. Warm up the air fryer to 375 °F.
5. Air fry the stuffed grape leaves for 15 minutes or 'til heated through.
6. Prepare and serve either warm or at room temp.

Per serving: Calories: 180kcal; Fat: 10g; Carbs: 22g; Protein: 3g

37. Air Fryer Caprese Skewers with Balsamic Glaze

Preparation time: 10 minutes
Cooking time: 5 minutes
Servings: 4 (16 skewers)
Ingredients:

- 16 cherry tomatoes
- 16 fresh mozzarella balls
- 16 fresh basil leaves
- Balsamic glaze for drizzling
- Salt and pepper as required

Directions:

1. Thread a cherry tomato, a mozzarella ball, and a basil leaf onto each skewer.
2. Warm up the air fryer to 375 °F.
3. Put skewers in to your air fryer basket.
4. Air fry for 5 minutes or 'til the mozzarella begins to melt.
5. Season using salt and pepper and drizzle with balsamic glaze prior to presenting.

Per serving: Calories: 150kcal; Fat: 10g; Carbs: 5g; Protein: 8g

38. Air Fryer Za'atar Pita Chips with Garlic Yogurt Dip

Preparation time: 10 minutes
Cooking time: 5 minutes
Servings: 4
Ingredients:

- 4 whole-wheat pita bread
- 2 tbsps. olive oil
- 2 tbsps. za'atar spice blend
- 1 tsp. garlic powder
- Salt as required
- 1 cup Greek yogurt
- 1 piece garlic, crushed

Directions:

1. Warm up the air fryer to 375 °F.
2. Cut pita bread into triangles.
3. In your bowl, toss pita triangles using olive oil, za'atar, garlic powder, and salt.
4. Air fry for 5 minutes or 'til the pita chips are crispy.
5. In your other bowl, mix Greek yogurt and crushed garlic to make the dip.
6. Serve the za'atar pita chips with garlic yogurt dip.

Per serving: Calories: 220kcal; Fat: 10g; Carbs: 28g; Protein: 6g

39. Crispy Eggplant Chips with Yogurt Dip

Preparation time: 20 minutes
Cooking time: 10 minutes
Servings: 4
Ingredients:

- 1 big eggplant, cut
- 1 cup breadcrumbs
- 1/2 cup grated Parmesan cheese
- 2 tsps. dried oregano
- Salt and pepper as required
- 1 cup Greek yogurt
- 1 tbsp. lemon juice
- 1 piece garlic, crushed

Directions:

1. Warm up the air fryer to 375 °F.
2. In your bowl, mix breadcrumbs, Parmesan cheese, dried oregano, salt, and pepper.
3. Dip eggplant slices into the breadcrumb mixture, covering all sides
4. Arrange the coated eggplant slices in to your air fryer basket.
5. Air fry for 10 minutes or 'til the eggplant is crispy.
6. In your separate bowl, mix Greek yogurt, lemon juice, and crushed garlic to make the dip.
7. Serve the crispy eggplant chips with yogurt dip.

Per serving: Calories: 250kcal; Fat: 10g; Carbs: 30g; Protein: 12g

40. Tomato and Basil Bruschetta Cups

Preparation time: 15 minutes
Cooking time: 5 minutes
Servings: 4 (12 cups)
Ingredients:

- 12 mini phyllo cups (store-bought)
- 1 cup cherry tomatoes, diced
- 1/4 cup fresh basil, chopped
- 2 tbsps. balsamic glaze
- 1 tbsp. olive oil
- Salt and pepper as required

Directions:

1. Warm up the air fryer to 375 °F.
2. In your bowl, mix salt, diced cherry tomatoes, fresh basil, balsamic glaze, olive oil, and pepper.
3. Put a spoonful of the mixture into each phyllo cup.
4. Air fry for 5 minutes or 'til the phyllo cups are golden brown.
5. Serve warm.

Per serving: Calories: 180kcal; Fat: 10g; Carbs: 20g; Protein: 4g

41. Spinach and Artichoke Stuffed Portobello Mushrooms

Preparation time: 15 minutes
Cooking time: 15 minutes
Servings: 4
Ingredients:

- 4 big portobello mushrooms, stems taken out
- 2 cups fresh spinach, chopped
- 1 can (14 oz) artichoke hearts, drained and chopped
- 1 cup vegan cream cheese
- 1/2 cup nutritional yeast
- 2 pieces garlic, crushed
- 1/4 cup fresh parsley, chopped
- Olive oil for brushing
- Salt and pepper as required

Directions:

1. Warm up the air fryer to 375 °F.
2. Brush the portobello mushrooms using olive oil and Season using salt and pepper.
3. In your bowl, mix together chopped spinach, chopped artichoke hearts, vegan cream cheese, nutritional yeast, crushed garlic, and fresh parsley.
4. Stuff each portobello mushroom with the spinach and artichoke mixture.
5. Place stuffed mushrooms in to your air fryer basket.
6. Air fry for 15 minutes or 'til the mushrooms are tender.
7. Serve as a savory and satisfying dish.

Per serving: Calories: 280kcal; Fat: 18g; Carbs: 20g; Protein: 10g

42. Air-Fried Walnut and Date Stuffed Figs

Preparation time: 10 minutes
Cooking time: 5 minutes
Servings: 4
Ingredients:

- 8 fresh figs
- 1/4 cup walnuts, chopped
- 1/4 cup dates, chopped
- 1 tbsp. honey
- 1/2 tsp. cinnamon

Directions:

1. Warm up the air fryer to 375 °F.
2. Make a small "X" cut into the top of every fig, taking care not to cut all the way through before beginning the cut.
3. In your bowl, mix chopped walnuts, chopped dates, honey, and cinnamon.
4. Gently pry open the figs and stuff each with the walnut and date mixture.
5. Place stuffed figs in to your air fryer basket.
6. Air fry for 4-5 minutes or 'til the figs are softened and the filling is warm.
7. Allow the stuffed figs to cool slightly prior to presenting.
8. Enjoy these warm and gooey Air-Fried Walnut and Date Stuffed Figs with a drizzle of honey.

Per serving: Calories: 150kcal; Fat: 5g; Carbs: 30g; Protein: 2g

43. Eggplant and Chickpea Stew

Preparation time: 10 minutes
Cooking time: 20 minutes
Servings: 4
Ingredients:

- 1 big eggplant, diced
- 1 can (15 oz) chickpeas
- 1 can (14 oz) diced tomatoes
- 1 onion, diced
- 2 pieces garlic, crushed
- 1 tsp. ground cumin
- 1 tsp. smoked paprika
- 1/2 tsp. ground coriander
- 1/2 cup vegetable broth
- Olive oil for brushing
- Fresh parsley for garnish
- Salt and pepper as required

Directions:

1. Warm up the air fryer to 375 °F.
2. In your bowl, toss diced eggplant using olive oil, salt, and pepper.
3. Put eggplant in to your air fryer basket then cook for 15 minutes or 'til softened and slightly browned.
4. In your big skillet, sauté diced onion and crushed garlic 'til softened.
5. Include chickpeas, diced tomatoes, ground cumin, smoked paprika, ground coriander, and vegetable broth to the skillet. Simmer for 5 minutes.
6. Stir in the air-fried eggplant.
7. Garnish with fresh parsley prior to presenting.
8. Serve the stew over rice or with crusty bread.

Per serving: Calories: 250kcal; Fat: 6g; Carbs: 40g; Protein: 10g

44. Vegan Moussaka

Preparation time: 10 minutes
Cooking time: 20 minutes
Servings: 4
Ingredients:

- 2 big eggplants, cut
- 1 cup lentils, cooked
- 1 onion, diced
- 2 pieces garlic, crushed
- 1 can (14 oz) diced tomatoes
- 1/4 cup tomato paste
- 1 tsp. dried oregano
- 1 tsp. ground cinnamon
- 1/2 cup vegan bechamel sauce
- Olive oil for brushing
- Salt and pepper as required

Directions:

1. Warm up the air fryer to 375 °F.
2. Brush eggplant slices using olive oil and Season using salt and pepper.
3. Air fry the eggplant slices for 8-10 minutes or 'til softened and slightly browned.
4. In your skillet, sauté diced onion and crushed garlic 'til softened.
5. Include cooked lentils, diced tomatoes, tomato paste, dried oregano, ground cinnamon, salt, and pepper. Simmer for 5 minutes.
6. In your oven-safe dish, layer the air-fried eggplant slices with the lentil mixture.
7. Pour vegan bechamel sauce over the top.
8. Air fry for an extra 10 minutes or 'til the moussaka is heated through and the top is golden brown.
9. Serve this vegan moussaka with a side salad.

Per serving: Calories: 350kcal; Fat: 12g; Carbs: 45g; Protein: 15g

45. Air-Fried Falafel Wrap with Tahini Sauce

Preparation time: 15 minutes
Cooking time: 15 minutes
Servings: 4
Ingredients:

- 1 can (15 oz) chickpeas
- 1/2 cup fresh parsley, chopped
- 1/4 cup red onion, finely chopped
- 2 pieces garlic, crushed
- 1 tsp. ground cumin
- 1 tsp. ground coriander
- 1/2 tsp. baking soda
- 1 tbsp. olive oil
- 4 whole-grain or gluten-free wraps
- Fresh veggies (lettuce, tomatoes, cucumbers) for filling
- Tahini sauce for drizzling

Directions:

1. In the blending container that you have, blend chickpeas, fresh parsley, red onion, crushed garlic, ground cumin, ground coriander, baking soda, and olive oil 'til a coarse mixture forms.
2. Form the mixture into small falafel balls.
3. Warm up the air fryer to 375 °F.
4. Air fry the falafel balls for 15 minutes or 'til golden and crispy.
5. Warm the wraps in to your air fryer for the last 2 minutes.
6. Assemble the wraps with falafel balls and fresh veggies.
7. Drizzle with tahini sauce prior to presenting.
8. Enjoy this quick and delicious air-fried falafel wrap.

Per serving: Calories: 350kcal; Fat: 12g; Carbs: 45g; Protein: 12g

46. Vegan Spanakopita with Dairy-Free Feta

Preparation time: 10 minutes
Cooking time: 20 minutes
Servings: 4
Ingredients:

- 1 package (10 oz) frozen chopped spinach
- 1 cup dairy-free feta cheese, crumbled
- 1/4 cup nutritional yeast
- 1 onion, finely chopped
- 2 pieces garlic, crushed
- 1/4 cup fresh dill, chopped
- 1 package (16 sheets) vegan phyllo dough
- Olive oil for brushing
- Salt and pepper as required

Directions:

1. Warm up the air fryer to 375 °F.
2. In your bowl, mix chopped spinach, dairy-free feta cheese, nutritional yeast, chopped onion, crushed garlic, fresh dill, salt, and pepper.
3. Lay out one sheet of vegan phyllo dough, brush using olive oil, and layer another sheet on top. Repeat 'til you have 4 layers.
4. Spoon the spinach and feta mixture along one edge of the phyllo dough.
5. Roll the phyllo dough to create a log, then coil it into a spiral shape.
6. Brush the top using olive oil.
7. Air fry for 20 minutes or 'til the phyllo is golden and crispy.
8. Serve this vegan spanakopita as a delightful appetizer or main dish.

Per serving: Calories: 280kcal; Fat: 15g; Carbs: 30g; Protein: 8g

47. Greek-style Stuffed Peppers with Rice and Vegetables

Preparation time: 10 minutes
Cooking time: 20 minutes
Servings: 4
Ingredients:

- 4 big bell peppers, divided and seeds taken out
- 1 cup cooked brown rice
- 1 can (15 oz) chickpeas
- 1 cup cherry tomatoes, diced
- 1/2 cup red onion, finely chopped
- 1/4 cup Kalamata olives, cut
- 1/4 cup fresh parsley, chopped
- 2 tbsps. olive oil
- 1 tsp. dried oregano
- Salt and pepper as required

Directions:

1. Warm up the air fryer to 375 °F.
2. In your bowl, mix cooked brown rice, chickpeas, cherry tomatoes, red onion, Kalamata olives, fresh parsley, olive oil, dried oregano, salt, and pepper.
3. Stuff each bell pepper half with the rice and vegetable mixture.
4. Arrange the stuffed peppers in to your air fryer basket.
5. Air fry for 20 minutes or 'til the peppers are tender.
6. Serve these Greek-style stuffed peppers as a satisfying and wholesome meal.

Per serving: Calories: 320kcal; Fat: 10g; Carbs: 50g; Protein: 10g

48. Mediterranean Roasted Vegetable Platter

Preparation time: 15 minutes
Cooking time: 15 minutes
Servings: 4
Ingredients:

- 1 eggplant, cut
- 1 zucchini, cut
- 1 red bell pepper, cut
- 1 yellow bell pepper, cut
- 1 red onion, cut
- 1 cup cherry tomatoes
- 2 tbsps. olive oil
- 1 tsp. dried oregano
- 1 tsp. dried thyme
- Salt and pepper as required
- Hummus for presenting

Directions:

1. Warm up the air fryer to 375 °F.
2. In your big bowl, toss yellow bell pepper, red onion, eggplant, zucchini, red bell pepper, and cherry tomatoes using olive oil, dried oregano, dried thyme, salt, and pepper.
3. Arrange the vegetables in a single layer in to your air fryer basket.
4. Fry the vegetables in an air fryer for 15 minutes, or until they are soft and have a mild caramelization.
5. Serve roasted vegetables on a platter with a side of hummus.
6. Enjoy this colorful and nutritious Mediterranean dish.

Per serving: Calories: 180kcal; Fat: 10g; Carbs: 20g; Protein: 4g

49. Air-Fried Honey Sesame Cinnamon Pita Chips

Preparation time: 10 minutes
Cooking time: 5 minutes
Servings: 4
Ingredients:

- 4 whole wheat pitas, cut into triangles
- 2 tbsps. olive oil
- 2 tbsps. honey
- 1 tsp. ground cinnamon
- 2 tbsps. sesame seeds
- Pinch of salt

Directions:

1. Warm up the air fryer to 350 °F.
2. In your bowl, mix olive oil, honey, ground cinnamon, sesame seeds, and a pinch of salt.
3. Toss the pita triangles in the honey and sesame mixture, ensuring they are well coated.
4. Place coated pita triangles in to your air fryer basket in a single layer.
5. Air fry for 4-5 minutes or 'til the pita chips are golden and crispy.
6. Allow the honey sesame cinnamon pita chips to cool prior to presenting.
7. Enjoy these sweet and crunchy pita chips as a delightful snack.

Per serving: Calories: 180kcal; Fat: 8g; Carbs: 25g; Protein: 3g

50. Ratatouille Stuffed Zucchini Boats

Preparation time: 10 minutes
Cooking time: 20 minutes
Servings: 4
Ingredients:

- 4 big zucchini, divided lengthwise
- 1 cup eggplant, diced
- 1 cup bell peppers, diced
- 1 cup cherry tomatoes, divided
- 1 onion, diced
- 2 pieces garlic, crushed
- 1/4 cup fresh basil, chopped
- 1/4 cup fresh thyme leaves
- 2 tbsps. tomato paste
- Olive oil for brushing
- Salt and pepper as required

Directions:

1. Warm up the air fryer to 375 °F.
2. Scoop out the center of each zucchini half, leaving a boat-like shape.
3. In your skillet, sauté diced eggplant, diced bell peppers, cherry tomatoes, diced onion, and crushed garlic 'til softened.
4. Stir in fresh basil, fresh thyme, tomato paste, salt, and pepper.
5. Brush the zucchini boats using olive oil and Season using salt and pepper.
6. Fill each zucchini boat with the ratatouille mixture.
7. Arrange the stuffed zucchini in to your air fryer basket.
8. Air fry for 20 minutes or 'til the zucchini is tender.
9. Serve these ratatouille stuffed zucchini boats as a delightful and healthy dish.

Per serving: Calories: 200kcal; Fat: 8g; Carbs: 30g; Protein: 6g

51. Stuffed Grape Leaves (Dolma) with Rice and Herbs

Preparation time: 10 minutes
Cooking time: 20 minutes
Servings: 4 (32 grape leaves)
Ingredients:

- 1 jar (16 oz) grape leaves in brine
- 1 cup white rice, cooked
- 1/2 cup pine nuts, toasted
- 1/4 cup fresh dill, chopped
- 1/4 cup fresh mint, chopped
- 1/4 cup fresh parsley, chopped
- 1/4 cup olive oil
- Juice of 2 lemons
- Salt and pepper as required

Directions:

1. Warm up the air fryer to 375 °F.
2. In your bowl, mix cooked white rice, toasted pine nuts, chopped dill, chopped mint, chopped parsley, olive oil, lemon juice, salt, and pepper.
3. Bring a grape leaf on a flat surface, vein side up.
4. Spoon a small amount of the rice mixture onto the middle of the leaf.
5. Fold sides of the leaf over your filling, then roll from the bottom to the top, creating a tight roll.
6. Proceed with the leftover grape leaves and fillings using the same method.
7. Arrange the stuffed grape leaves in to your air fryer basket.
8. Air fry for 20 minutes or 'til the grape leaves are heated through.
9. Serve these stuffed grape leaves as a delightful appetizer or side dish.

Per serving: Calories: 220kcal; Fat: 12g; Carbs: 25g; Protein: 4g

52. Mediterranean Quinoa Salad with Roasted Vegetables

Preparation time: 10 minutes
Cooking time: 20 minutes
Servings: 4
Ingredients:

- 1 cup quinoa, washed
- 2 cups cherry tomatoes, divided
- 1 zucchini, diced
- 1 red bell pepper, diced
- 1 red onion, cut
- 1/4 cup Kalamata olives, cut
- 1/4 cup fresh parsley, chopped
- 2 tbsps. olive oil
- Juice of 1 lemon
- Salt and pepper as required

Directions:

1. Warm up the air fryer to 400 °F.
2. In your bowl, toss cherry tomatoes, zucchini, red bell pepper, and red onion using olive oil, salt, and pepper.
3. Disperse vegetables in a single layer in to your air fryer basket and roast for 15 minutes or 'til tender.
4. While the vegetables are roasting, cook quinoa according to package instructions.
5. In your big bowl, combine cooked quinoa, roasted vegetables, Kalamata olives, fresh parsley, and lemon juice.
6. Toss everything together then adjust seasoning if needed.
7. Serve as a refreshing and nutritious salad.

Per serving: Calories: 300kcal; Fat: 10g; Carbs: 45g; Protein: 10g

53. Vegan Spinach and Artichoke Dip

Preparation time: 10 minutes
Cooking time: 15 minutes
Servings: 4
Ingredients:

- 1 cup raw cashews, soaked in a hot water for 1 hour
- 1 cup unsweetened almond milk
- 1 cup frozen chopped spinach
- 1 can (14 oz) artichoke hearts, drained and chopped
- 1/4 cup nutritional yeast
- 2 pieces garlic, crushed
- 1 tbsp. lemon juice
- Salt and pepper as required

Directions:

1. Warm up the air fryer to 375 °F.
2. In your blender, combine soaked cashews and almond milk. Blend 'til smooth.
3. In your bowl, mix the cashew cream, chopped spinach, chopped artichoke hearts, nutritional yeast, crushed garlic, lemon juice, salt, and pepper.
4. Put the mixture in a dish that can be placed in the oven.
5. Air fry for 15 minutes or 'til the dip is hot and bubbly.
6. Serve vegan spinach and artichoke dip with veggie sticks or pita chips.

Per serving: Calories: 220kcal; Fat: 15g; Carbs: 18g; Protein: 8g

54. Vegan Eggplant Caponata with Crispy Pita

Preparation time: 15 minutes
Cooking time: 15 minutes
Servings: 4
Ingredients:

- 1 big eggplant, diced
- 1 can (14 oz) diced tomatoes
- 1/2 cup Kalamata olives, cut
- 1/4 cup capers, drained
- 1/4 cup red onion, finely chopped
- 2 pieces garlic, crushed
- 2 tbsps. red wine vinegar
- 2 tbsps. olive oil
- 1 tsp. dried oregano
- Salt and pepper as required
- 4 whole-grain or gluten-free pitas, toasted

Directions:

1. Warm up the air fryer to 375 °F.
2. In your bowl, combine diced eggplant, diced tomatoes, cut Kalamata olives, capers, chopped red onion, crushed garlic, red wine vinegar, olive oil, dried oregano, salt, and pepper.
3. Disperse the mixture in a single layer in to your air fryer basket.
4. Air fry for 15 minutes or 'til the eggplant is tender and slightly caramelized.
5. Toast the pitas in to your air fryer for the last 2 minutes.
6. Serve the vegan eggplant caponata over crispy pita.
7. Enjoy this flavorful and satisfying dish.

Per serving: Calories: 280kcal; Fat: 12g; Carbs: 40g; Protein: 8g

55. Greek Lemon Garlic Roasted Potatoes

Preparation time: 10 minutes
Cooking time: 20 minutes
Servings: 4
Ingredients:

- 4 big potatoes, cut into wedges
- 1/4 cup olive oil
- Juice of 2 lemons
- 4 pieces garlic, crushed
- 1 tsp. dried oregano
- Salt and pepper as required
- Fresh parsley for garnish

Directions:

1. Warm up the air fryer to 400 °F.
2. In your bowl, toss potato wedges using olive oil, lemon juice, crushed garlic, dried oregano, salt, and pepper.
3. Disperse potato wedges in a one layer in to your air fryer basket.
4. Air fry for 20 minutes or 'til the potatoes are golden and crispy.
5. Garnish with fresh parsley prior to presenting.
6. Enjoy these Greek-style lemon garlic roasted potatoes as a flavorful side dish.

Per serving: Calories: 250kcal; Fat: 10g; Carbs: 35g; Protein: 5g

56. Air Fryer Sweet Potato and Chickpea Buddha Bowl

Preparation time: 15 minutes
Cooking time: 15 minutes
Servings: 4
Ingredients:

- 2 sweet potatoes, skinned and cubed
- 1 can (15 oz) chickpeas
- 2 tbsps. olive oil
- 1 tsp. ground cumin
- 1 tsp. smoked paprika
- 1/2 tsp. ground turmeric
- 4 cups mixed greens
- 1 avocado, cut
- 1/4 cup tahini dressing
- Salt and pepper as required

Directions:

1. Warm up the air fryer to 400 °F.
2. In your bowl, toss sweet potato cubes and chickpeas using olive oil, ground cumin, smoked paprika, ground turmeric, salt, and pepper.
3. Disperse the sweet potatoes and chickpeas in a single layer in to your air fryer basket.
4. Air fry for 15 minutes or 'til the sweet potatoes are tender then chickpeas are crispy.
5. Assemble the Buddha bowls with mixed greens, air-fried sweet potatoes, air-fried chickpeas, cut avocado, and a drizzle of tahini dressing.
6. Enjoy this nourishing and delicious Buddha bowl.

Per serving: Calories: 400kcal; Fat: 20g; Carbs: 50g; Protein: 10g

57. Spinach and Olive Vegan Stuffed Mushrooms

Preparation time: 15 minutes
Cooking time: 15 minutes
Servings: 4 (16 mushrooms)
Ingredients:

- 16 big button mushrooms, stems taken out and chopped
- 1 cup fresh spinach, chopped
- 1/4 cup Kalamata olives, finely chopped
- 1/4 cup vegan breadcrumbs
- 1/4 cup nutritional yeast
- 2 pieces garlic, crushed
- 2 tbsps. olive oil
- 1 tbsp. fresh parsley, chopped
- Salt and pepper as required

Directions:

1. Warm up the air fryer to 375 °F.
2. In your skillet, sauté chopped mushroom stems, chopped fresh spinach, finely chopped Kalamata olives, crushed garlic, and olive oil 'til the spinach is wilted.
3. In your bowl, combine the sautéed mixture with vegan breadcrumbs, nutritional yeast, chopped fresh parsley, salt, and pepper.
4. Fill each mushroom cap with using stuffing mixture.
5. Arrange the stuffed mushrooms in to your air fryer basket.
6. Air fry for 15 minutes or 'til the mushrooms are tender then the stuffing is golden.
7. Serve these spinach and olive vegan stuffed mushrooms as a delightful appetizer.

Per serving: Calories: 120kcal; Fat: 8g; Carbs: 10g; Protein: 5g

58. Mediterranean Quinoa-stuffed Bell Peppers

Preparation time: 10 minutes
Cooking time: 20 minutes
Servings: 4
Ingredients:

- 4 big bell peppers, divided and seeds taken out
- 1 cup cooked quinoa
- 1 can (15 oz) chickpeas
- 1 cup cherry tomatoes, diced
- 1/2 cup Kalamata olives, cut
- 1/4 cup fresh parsley, chopped
- 2 tbsps. olive oil
- 1 tsp. dried oregano
- Salt and pepper as required

Directions:

1. Warm up the air fryer to 375 °F.
2. In your bowl, mix cooked quinoa, chickpeas, cherry tomatoes, Kalamata olives, fresh parsley, olive oil, dried oregano, salt, and pepper.
3. Stuff each bell pepper half using the quinoa mixture.
4. Arrange the stuffed peppers in to your air fryer basket.
5. Air fry for 20 minutes or 'til the peppers are tender.
6. Serve these Mediterranean quinoa-stuffed bell peppers as a wholesome and flavorful dish.

Per serving: Calories: 320kcal; Fat: 12g; Carbs: 45g; Protein: 10g

59. Air-Fried Greek Zucchini Fritters

Preparation time: 15 minutes
Cooking time: 15 minutes
Servings: 4
Ingredients:

- 2 big zucchinis, grated and squeezed to remove excess moisture
- 1/2 cup breadcrumbs
- 1/4 cup fresh mint, chopped
- 1/4 cup fresh dill, chopped
- 1/4 cup red onion, finely chopped
- 1/4 cup vegan feta cheese, crumbled
- 1 flax egg (with 1 tbsp. ground flaxseed mixed with 3 tbsps. water)
- Olive oil for brushing
- Vegan tzatziki sauce for dipping
- Salt and pepper as required

Directions:

1. Warm up the air fryer to 375 °F.
2. In your bowl, combine grated zucchini, breadcrumbs, chopped fresh mint, chopped fresh dill, chopped red onion, vegan feta cheese, flax egg, salt, and pepper.
3. Form the mixture into small fritters.
4. Brush the fritters using olive oil.
5. Air fry for 15 minutes or 'til the zucchini fritters are golden and crispy.
6. Serve these air-fried Greek zucchini fritters with vegan tzatziki sauce for dipping.
7. Enjoy this tasty and light appetizer.

Per serving: Calories: 180kcal; Fat: 8g; Carbs: 25g; Protein: 6g

60. Vegan Mediterranean Cauliflower Steaks

Preparation time: 10 minutes
Cooking time: 20 minutes
Servings: 4
Ingredients:

- 1 big cauliflower head, cut into steaks
- 1/4 cup olive oil
- 2 tbsps. lemon juice
- 2 pieces garlic, crushed
- 1 tsp. dried oregano
- 1 tsp. smoked paprika
- Salt and pepper as required
- Fresh parsley for garnish

Directions:

1. Warm up the air fryer to 375 °F.
2. In your bowl, whisk together olive oil, lemon juice, crushed garlic, dried oregano, smoked paprika, salt, and pepper.
3. Brush both sides of the cauliflower steaks using the marinade.
4. Arrange the cauliflower steaks in a single layer in to your air fryer basket.
5. Air fry for 20 minutes or 'til the cauliflower steaks are tender and golden.
6. Garnish with fresh parsley prior to presenting.
7. Serve these vegan Mediterranean cauliflower steaks as a satisfying and flavorful main dish.

Per serving: Calories: 150kcal; Fat: 12g; Carbs: 10g; Protein: 5g

FISH AND SEAFOOD

61. Garlic Butter Lemon Shrimp Skewers

Preparation time: 15 minutes
Cooking time: 8 minutes
Servings: 4
Ingredients:

- 1 lb. big shrimp, skinned and deveined
- 3 tbsps. unsalted butter, melted
- 3 pieces garlic, crushed
- Zest of 1 lemon
- Juice of 1 lemon
- 1 tbsp. fresh parsley, chopped
- Salt and pepper as required

Directions:

1. Warm up the air fryer to 400 °F.
2. In your bowl, toss shrimp with melted butter, crushed garlic, lemon zest, lemon juice, chopped fresh parsley, salt, and pepper.
3. Thread the shrimp onto skewers.
4. Arrange the skewers in to your air fryer basket.
5. Air fry for 8 minutes or 'til the shrimp are pink then cooked through.
6. Serve these garlic butter lemon shrimp skewers as a succulent and flavorful appetizer or main dish.

Per serving: Calories: 200kcal; Fat: 10g; Carbs: 3g; Protein: 25g

62. Mediterranean Baked Haddock with Olives

Preparation time: 15 minutes
Cooking time: 15 minutes
Servings: 4
Ingredients:

- 4 haddock fillets
- 1/2 cup cherry tomatoes, divided
- 1/4 cup Kalamata olives, cut
- 2 tbsps. olive oil
- 2 pieces garlic, crushed
- 1 tsp. dried oregano
- Salt and pepper as required
- Lemon wedges for presenting

Directions:

1. Warm up the air fryer to 375 °F.
2. Place haddock fillets in a baking dish.
3. In your bowl, toss cherry tomatoes with cut Kalamata olives, olive oil, crushed garlic, dried oregano, salt, and pepper.
4. Disperse the tomato mixture over the haddock fillets.
5. Cover the baking dish with foil.
6. Air fry for 15 minutes or 'til the haddock is flaky.
7. Serve with your lemon wedges for added freshness.
8. Enjoy this Mediterranean baked haddock as a light and nutritious meal.

Per serving: Calories: 180kcal; Fat: 8g; Carbs: 4g; Protein: 25g

63. Air Fryer Salmon with Dill and Lemon

Preparation time: 10 minutes
Cooking time: 12 minutes
Servings: 4
Ingredients:

- 4 salmon fillets
- 2 tbsps. olive oil
- 1 tbsp. fresh dill, chopped
- 1 tsp. lemon zest
- 1 tbsp. lemon juice
- 1/2 tsp. garlic powder
- Salt and pepper as required
- Lemon wedges for presenting

Directions:

1. Warm up the air fryer to 375 °F.
2. Brush salmon fillets using olive oil and put them in to your air fryer basket.
3. In your small bowl, mix chopped fresh dill, lemon zest, lemon juice, garlic powder, salt, and pepper.
4. Disperse the dill mixture over the salmon fillets.
5. Air fry for 12 minutes or 'til the salmon is cooked to your liking.
6. Serve with your lemon wedges for an extra burst of citrus flavor.
7. Enjoy this quick and delicious air-fried salmon.

Per serving: Calories: 250kcal; Fat: 15g; Carbs: 2g; Protein: 25g

64. Greek-style Shrimp and Feta Orzo

Preparation time: 15 minutes
Cooking time: 15 minutes
Servings: 4
Ingredients:

- 1 cup orzo pasta, cooked
- 1 lb. big shrimp, skinned and deveined
- 2 tbsps. olive oil
- 3 pieces garlic, crushed
- 1 can (14 oz) diced tomatoes, drained
- 1/2 cup Kalamata olives, cut
- 1 tsp. dried oregano
- 1/2 cup crumbled feta cheese
- Fresh parsley for garnish
- Salt and pepper as required

Directions:

1. Warm up the air fryer to 400 °F.
2. In your bowl, toss cooked orzo with shrimp, olive oil, crushed garlic, diced tomatoes, cut Kalamata olives, dried oregano, crumbled feta cheese, salt, and pepper.
3. Disperse the mixture in to your air fryer basket.
4. Air fry for 15 minutes or 'til the shrimp are pink and orzo is heated through.
5. Garnish with fresh parsley prior to presenting.
6. Serve this Greek-style shrimp and feta orzo as a complete and satisfying meal.

Per serving: Calories: 350kcal; Fat: 12g; Carbs: 35g; Protein: 25g

65. Roasted Red Pepper and Feta Stuffed Squid

Preparation time: 15 minutes
Cooking time: 15 minutes
Servings: 4
Ingredients:

- 8 small squid tubes, cleaned
- 1/2 cup crumbled feta cheese
- 1/4 cup roasted red peppers, chopped
- 2 tbsps. fresh parsley, chopped
- 1 tbsp. olive oil
- 1 tsp. lemon zest
- 1/2 tsp. dried oregano
- Salt and pepper as required
- Lemon wedges for presenting

Directions:

1. Warm up the air fryer to 375 °F.
2. In your bowl, mix crumbled feta cheese, chopped roasted red peppers, chopped fresh parsley, olive oil, lemon zest, dried oregano, salt, and pepper.
3. Stuff each squid tube with the feta mixture.
4. Secure the ends with toothpicks.
5. Arrange the stuffed squid in to your air fryer basket.
6. Air fry for 15 minutes or 'til the squid is cooked and lightly golden.
7. Serve with your lemon wedges for added zest.
8. Enjoy these roasted red pepper and feta stuffed squid as an elegant seafood dish.

Per serving: Calories: 180kcal; Fat: 8g; Carbs: 8g; Protein: 20g

66. Lemon Garlic Herb Air-Fried Shrimp

Preparation time: 10 minutes
Cooking time: 8 minutes
Servings: 4
Ingredients:

- 1 lb. big shrimp, skinned and deveined
- 2 tbsps. olive oil
- 3 pieces garlic, crushed
- 1 tbsp. fresh parsley, chopped
- 1 tsp. lemon zest
- 1 tbsp. lemon juice
- 1/2 tsp. dried oregano
- Salt and pepper as required

Directions:

1. Warm up the air fryer to 400 °F.
2. In your bowl, toss shrimp using olive oil, crushed garlic, chopped fresh parsley, lemon zest, lemon juice, dried oregano, salt, and pepper.
3. Disperse shrimp in a single layer in to your air fryer basket.
4. Air fry for 8 minutes or 'til the shrimp are pink then cooked through.
5. Serve these lemon garlic herb air-fried shrimp as a quick and flavorful seafood dish.

Per serving: Calories: 180kcal; Fat: 8g; Carbs: 2g; Protein: 25g

67. Grilled Swordfish Steaks with Olive Tapenade

Preparation time: 15 minutes
Cooking time: 10 minutes
Servings: 4
Ingredients:

- 4 swordfish steaks
- 2 tbsps. olive oil
- 1 tbsp. lemon juice
- 2 pieces garlic, crushed
- 1 tsp. dried oregano
- Salt and pepper as required
- Olive tapenade for topping

Directions:

1. Warm up the air fryer to 400 °F.
2. In your bowl, whisk together salt, olive oil, lemon juice, crushed garlic, dried oregano, and pepper.
3. Brush both sides of the swordfish steaks using the marinade.
4. Arrange the steaks in to your air fryer basket.
5. Air fry for 10 minutes or 'til the swordfish is cooked through and has a grilled appearance.
6. Top the swordfish steaks with olive tapenade prior to presenting.
7. Enjoy these grilled swordfish steaks with a burst of Mediterranean flavors.

Per serving: Calories: 250kcal; Fat: 12g; Carbs: 2g; Protein: 30g

68. Air Fryer Crab Cakes with Remoulade Sauce

Preparation time: 20 minutes
Cooking time: 10 minutes
Servings: 4
Ingredients:

- 1 lb. lump crabmeat, drained
- 1/4 cup mayonnaise
- 1 tbsp. Dijon mustard
- 1 tbsp. Worcestershire sauce
- 1/4 cup breadcrumbs
- 2 tbsps. fresh parsley, chopped
- 1 tsp. Old Bay seasoning
- 1/2 tsp. garlic powder
- Salt and pepper as required
- 1 egg, beaten
- Olive oil spray
- Remoulade sauce for dipping

Directions:

1. In your bowl, mix lump crabmeat, mayonnaise, Dijon mustard, Worcestershire sauce, breadcrumbs, chopped fresh parsley, Old Bay seasoning, garlic powder, salt, and pepper.
2. Gently fold in the beaten egg to bind the mixture.
3. Form crab cakes and put them on a parchment-lined tray.
4. Warm up the air fryer to 375 °F.
5. Mildly spray the crab cakes using olive oil.
6. Air fry for 10 minutes or 'til the crab cakes are golden then cooked through.
7. Serve these air fryer crab cakes with remoulade sauce for a delicious seafood treat.
8. Enjoy the crispy exterior and flavorful interior of these crab cakes.

Per serving: Calories: 200kcal; Fat: 10g; Carbs: 8g; Protein: 20g

69. Air-Fried Mediterranean Scallops

Preparation time: 10 minutes
Cooking time: 8 minutes
Servings: 4
Ingredients:

- 1 lb. sea scallops, patted dry
- 2 tbsps. olive oil
- 2 pieces garlic, crushed
- 1 tsp. dried oregano
- 1/2 tsp. smoked paprika
- Salt and pepper as required
- Lemon wedges for presenting

Directions:

1. Warm up the air fryer to 375 °F.
2. In your bowl, toss sea scallops using olive oil, crushed garlic, dried oregano, smoked paprika, salt, and pepper.
3. Disperse the scallops in a single layer in to your air fryer basket.
4. Air fry for 8 minutes or 'til the scallops are golden and opaque.
5. Serve lemon wedges for a burst of citrus flavor.
6. Enjoy these air-fried Mediterranean scallops as an elegant seafood dish.

Per serving: Calories: 150kcal; Fat: 8g; Carbs: 3g; Protein: 18g

70. Air-Fried Fish and Chips with Greek Yogurt Tartar Sauce

Preparation time: 15 minutes
Cooking time: 15 minutes
Servings: 4
Ingredients:

- 1 lb. white fish fillets (cod or haddock)
- 1 cup panko breadcrumbs
- 1/4 cup grated Parmesan cheese
- 1 tsp. dried oregano
- 1 tsp. paprika
- Salt and pepper as required
- Olive oil spray
- 4 big potatoes, cut into fries
- Greek Yogurt Tartar Sauce for dipping

Directions:

1. Warm up the air fryer to 400 °F.
2. In your bowl, mix panko breadcrumbs, grated Parmesan cheese, dried oregano, paprika, salt, and pepper.
3. Coat fish fillets with the breadcrumb mixture.
4. Place coated fish fillets in to your air fryer basket.
5. Mildly spray the fillets using olive oil.
6. Arrange the potato fries around the fish in the basket.
7. Air fry for 15 minutes or 'til the fish is golden and the fries are crispy.
8. Serve with Greek Yogurt Tartar Sauce for a tangy and creamy dip.
9. Enjoy this healthier version of Fish and Chips with a Mediterranean twist.

Per serving: Calories: 350kcal; Fat: 12g; Carbs: 40g; Protein: 20g

71. Herb-Crusted Air Fryer Tilapia

Preparation time: 10 minutes
Cooking time: 12 minutes
Servings: 4
Ingredients:

- 4 tilapia fillets
- 2 tbsps. olive oil
- 1/4 cup breadcrumbs
- 2 tbsps. fresh parsley, chopped
- 1 tbsp. fresh dill, chopped
- 1 tsp. lemon zest
- 1/2 tsp. garlic powder
- Salt and pepper as required
- Lemon wedges for presenting

Directions:

1. Warm up the air fryer to 400 °F.
2. Brush tilapia fillets using olive oil.
3. In your bowl, mix breadcrumbs, chopped fresh parsley, chopped fresh dill, lemon zest, garlic powder, salt, and pepper.
4. Press herb mixture onto both sides of each tilapia fillet.
5. Arrange the fillets in to your air fryer basket.
6. Air fry for 12 minutes or 'til the tilapia is golden and flakes easily.
7. Serve with your lemon wedges for added brightness.
8. Enjoy this herb-crusted air fryer tilapia as a light and flavorful dish.

Per serving: Calories: 180kcal; Fat: 8g; Carbs: 5g; Protein: 25g

72. Grilled Sardines with Lemon and Oregano

Preparation time: 15 minutes
Cooking time: 8 minutes
Servings: 4
Ingredients:

- 8 fresh sardines, cleaned and gutted
- 2 tbsps. olive oil
- Zest and juice of 1 lemon
- 1 tsp. dried oregano
- Salt and pepper as required
- Lemon wedges for presenting

Directions:

1. Warm up the air fryer to 400 °F.
2. Make diagonal cuts on both sides of each sardine.
3. In your bowl, mix olive oil, lemon zest, lemon juice, dried oregano, salt, and pepper.
4. Brush the sardines with the lemon and oregano mixture.
5. Arrange the sardines in to your air fryer basket.
6. Air fry for 8 minutes or 'til the sardines are golden then cooked through.
7. Serve with your lemon wedges for a citrusy touch.
8. Enjoy these grilled sardines with lemon and oregano as a flavorful seafood dish.

Per serving: Calories: 180kcal; Fat: 10g; Carbs: 2g; Protein: 20g

73. Spicy Harissa Grilled Prawns

Preparation time: 15 minutes
Cooking time: 8 minutes
Servings: 4
Ingredients:

- 1 lb. big prawns, skinned and deveined
- 2 tbsps. harissa paste
- 2 tbsps. olive oil
- 1 tsp. smoked paprika
- 1/2 tsp. cayenne pepper
- 1/2 tsp. garlic powder
- Salt and pepper as required
- Lemon wedges for presenting

Directions:

1. Warm up the air fryer to 400 °F.
2. In your bowl, mix harissa paste, olive oil, smoked paprika, cayenne pepper, garlic powder, salt, and pepper.
3. Toss prawns with the harissa mixture.
4. Arrange the prawns in to your air fryer basket.
5. Air fry for 8 minutes or 'til the prawns are pink then cooked through.
6. Serve with your lemon wedges for a zesty touch.
7. Enjoy these spicy harissa grilled prawns for a flavorful appetizer or main dish.

Per serving: Calories: 200kcal; Fat: 10g; Carbs: 2g; Protein: 25g

74. Baked Lemon Garlic Herb Salmon Pockets

Preparation time: 15 minutes
Cooking time: 12 minutes
Servings: 4
Ingredients:

- 4 salmon fillets
- 2 tbsps. olive oil
- Zest and juice of 1 lemon
- 3 pieces garlic, crushed
- 1 tbsp. fresh dill, chopped
- 1 tsp. dried thyme
- Salt and pepper as required
- Parchment paper for wrapping

Directions:

1. Warm up the air fryer to 375 °F.
2. In your bowl, mix olive oil, lemon zest, lemon juice, crushed garlic, chopped fresh dill, dried thyme, salt, and pepper.
3. Place each salmon fillet on a piece of your parchment paper.
4. Spoon the lemon garlic herb mixture over each fillet.
5. Fold and seal the parchment paper to create a pocket for each salmon fillet.
6. Arrange the salmon pockets in to your air fryer basket.
7. Air fry for 12 minutes or 'til the salmon is cooked through.
8. Serve these baked lemon garlic herb salmon pockets for a light and flavorful meal.
9. Enjoy the juicy and aromatic salmon with minimal effort.

Per serving: Calories: 250kcal; Fat: 15g; Carbs: 2g; Protein: 25g

75. Greek Lemon Butter Shrimp Skewers

Preparation time: 15 minutes
Cooking time: 8 minutes
Servings: 4
Ingredients:

- 1 lb. big shrimp, skinned and deveined
- 4 tbsps. unsalted butter, melted
- Zest and juice of 1 lemon
- 1 tsp. dried oregano
- 1 tsp. dried thyme
- 1/2 tsp. garlic powder
- Salt and pepper as required
- Lemon wedges for presenting

Directions:

1. Warm up the air fryer to 375 °F.
2. Thread shrimp onto skewers.
3. In your bowl, mix melted butter, lemon zest, lemon juice, dried oregano, dried thyme, garlic powder, salt, and pepper.
4. Brush the shrimp skewers with the lemon butter mixture.
5. Arrange the skewers in to your air fryer basket.
6. Air fry for 8 minutes or 'til the shrimp are pink then cooked through.
7. Serve with your lemon wedges for an extra burst of citrus flavor.
8. Enjoy these Greek lemon butter shrimp skewers as a succulent appetizer or main dish.

Per serving: Calories: 220kcal; Fat: 15g; Carbs: 2g; Protein: 20g

76. Air-Fried Coconut Shrimp with Mango Salsa

Preparation time: 20 minutes
Cooking time: 10 minutes
Servings: 4
Ingredients:

- 1 lb. big shrimp, skinned and deveined
- 1 cup shredded coconut
- 1 cup panko breadcrumbs
- 2 eggs, beaten
- Salt and pepper as required
- Olive oil spray
- Mango salsa for dipping

Directions:

1. Warm up the air fryer to 375 °F.
2. In separate bowls, place shredded coconut and panko breadcrumbs.
3. Dip each shrimp in beaten eggs, then coat with shredded coconut and panko mixture.
4. Place coated shrimp in a single layer in to your air fryer basket.
5. Mildly spray the shrimp using olive oil.
6. Air fry for 10 minutes or 'til the coconut shrimp are golden and crispy.
7. Serve with mango salsa for a tropical and sweet flavor.
8. Enjoy these air-fried coconut shrimp with mango salsa as a delightful appetizer.

Per serving: Calories: 250kcal; Fat: 12g; Carbs: 20g; Protein: 15g

77. Mediterranean Baked Cod with Cherry Tomatoes

Preparation time: 10 minutes
Cooking time: 15 minutes
Servings: 4
Ingredients:

- 4 cod fillets
- 1 cup cherry tomatoes, divided
- 2 tbsps. olive oil
- 2 pieces garlic, crushed
- 1 tsp. dried oregano
- 1/2 tsp. smoked paprika
- Salt and pepper as required
- Fresh basil for garnish

Directions:

1. Warm up the air fryer to 375 °F.
2. Put cod fillets in a baking dish.
3. In your bowl, toss cherry tomatoes using olive oil, crushed garlic, dried oregano, smoked paprika, salt, and pepper.
4. Disperse the tomato mixture over the cod fillets.
5. Cover the baking dish with foil.
6. Air fry for 15 minutes or 'til the cod is flaky.
7. Garnish with fresh basil prior to presenting.
8. Enjoy this light and flavorful Mediterranean baked cod.

Per serving: Calories: 200kcal; Fat: 8g; Carbs: 4g; Protein: 30g

78. Mediterranean Stuffed Mussels with Herbs

Preparation time: 15 minutes
Cooking time: 8 minutes
Servings: 4
Ingredients:

- 20 fresh mussels, cleaned and debearded
- 1/2 cup breadcrumbs
- 2 tbsps. fresh parsley, chopped
- 2 tbsps. fresh oregano, chopped
- 2 pieces garlic, crushed
- 2 tbsps. olive oil
- Lemon wedges for presenting

Directions:

1. Warm up the air fryer to 375 °F.
2. In your bowl, mix breadcrumbs, chopped fresh parsley, chopped fresh oregano, crushed garlic, and olive oil.
3. Spoon the breadcrumb mixture onto each mussel.
4. Arrange the stuffed mussels in to your air fryer basket.
5. Air fry for 8 minutes or 'til the mussels are cooked through.
6. Serve with your lemon wedges for a zesty touch.
7. Enjoy these Mediterranean stuffed mussels with herbs as a tasty seafood appetizer.

Per serving: Calories: 150kcal; Fat: 8g; Carbs: 10g; Protein: 10g

79. Shrimp and Spinach Stuffed Squid Tubes

Preparation time: 15 minutes
Cooking time: 15 minutes
Servings: 4
Ingredients:

- 8 small squid tubes, cleaned
- 1/2 lb. shrimp, skinned and deveined, chopped
- 2 cups fresh spinach, chopped
- 2 pieces garlic, crushed
- 2 tbsps. olive oil
- Zest and juice of 1 lemon
- 1 tsp. dried oregano
- Salt and pepper as required
- Lemon wedges for presenting

Directions:

1. Warm up the air fryer to 375 °F.
2. In your pan, sauté chopped shrimp, chopped fresh spinach, crushed garlic, olive oil, lemon zest, lemon juice, dried oregano, salt, and pepper 'til the shrimp are cooked then the spinach is wilted.
3. Stuff each squid tube with the shrimp and spinach mixture.
4. Secure the ends with toothpicks.
5. Arrange the stuffed squid in to your air fryer basket.
6. Air fry for 15 minutes or 'til the squid is cooked and lightly golden.
7. Serve with your lemon wedges for added zest.
8. Enjoy these shrimp and spinach stuffed squid tubes as an elegant seafood dish.

Per serving: Calories: 200kcal; Fat: 10g; Carbs: 5g; Protein: 20g

80. Garlic and Herb Grilled Clams

Preparation time: 15 minutes
Cooking time: 8 minutes
Servings: 4
Ingredients:

- 24 fresh clams, cleaned
- 2 tbsps. olive oil
- 2 pieces garlic, crushed
- 1 tbsp. fresh parsley, chopped
- 1 tsp. dried oregano
- 1/2 tsp. red pepper flakes (optional)
- Salt and pepper as required
- Lemon wedges for presenting

Directions:

1. Warm up the air fryer to 400 °F.
2. In your bowl, mix olive oil, crushed garlic, chopped fresh parsley, dried oregano, red pepper flakes (if using), salt, and pepper.
3. Toss the clams with the garlic and herb mixture.
4. Arrange the clams in to your air fryer basket.
5. Air fry for 8 minutes or 'til the clams are open then cooked.
6. Serve with your lemon wedges for added brightness.
7. Enjoy these garlic and herb grilled clams as a delicious seafood appetizer.

Per serving: Calories: 180kcal; Fat: 10g; Carbs: 4g; Protein: 20g

 # POULTRY AND MEAT

81. Italian Herb Crusted Pork Tenderloin

Preparation time: 10 minutes
Cooking time: 20 minutes
Servings: 4
Ingredients:

- 1 pork tenderloin
- 2 tbsps. olive oil
- 1 tbsp. dried Italian herbs (basil, oregano, thyme)
- 1 tsp. garlic powder
- Salt and pepper as required

Directions:

1. Warm up the air fryer to 400 °F.
2. In your bowl, mix olive oil, dried Italian herbs, garlic powder, salt, and pepper.
3. Coat the pork tenderloin with the Italian herb mixture.
4. Place pork tenderloin in to your air fryer basket.
5. Air fry for 20 minutes or 'til the pork is cooked through and has a golden crust.
6. Prior to cutting it, allow it to rest for a couple of precious minutes.
7. Serve this Italian herb crusted pork tenderloin for a flavorful and tender dish.
8. Enjoy the herb-infused taste of Italy in every bite.

Per serving: Calories: 250kcal; Fat: 10g; Carbs: 1g; Protein: 35g

82. Air Fryer Lamb Kofta Skewers

Preparation time: 18 minutes
Cooking time: 12 minutes
Servings: 4
Ingredients:

- 1 lb. ground lamb
- 1/4 cup breadcrumbs
- 1 small onion, grated
- 2 pieces garlic, crushed
- 1 tsp. ground cumin
- 1 tsp. ground coriander
- 1 tsp. smoked paprika
- Salt and pepper as required
- Wooden skewers, soaked in water
- Tahini sauce for dipping

Directions:

1. Warm up the air fryer to 375 °F.
2. In your bowl, mix ground lamb, breadcrumbs, grated onion, crushed garlic, ground cumin, ground coriander, smoked paprika, salt, and pepper.
3. Form the mixture into kofta shapes and thread onto soaked wooden skewers.
4. Arrange the lamb kofta skewers in to your air fryer basket.
5. Air fry for 12 minutes or 'til the koftas are cooked through and slightly browned.
6. Serve with tahini sauce for a delightful Middle Eastern flavor.
7. Enjoy these air fryer lamb kofta skewers as a tasty and satisfying dish.

Per serving: Calories: 400kcal; Fat: 30g; Carbs: 10g; Protein: 20g

83. Greek-style Chicken Pita Wraps with Tahini Sauce

Preparation time: 15 minutes
Cooking time: 15 minutes
Servings: 4
Ingredients:

- 1 lb. boneless, skinless chicken breasts, cut
- 2 tbsps. olive oil
- 1 tsp. dried oregano
- 1 tsp. dried thyme
- 1 tsp. garlic powder
- Salt and pepper as required
- 4 whole wheat pita bread
- Tzatziki or Tahini sauce for dressing
- Sliced cucumbers, tomatoes, and red onions for filling

Directions:

1. Warm up the air fryer to 375 °F.
2. In your bowl, mix olive oil, dried oregano, dried thyme, garlic powder, salt, and pepper.
3. Coat chicken slices with the Greek herb mixture.
4. Arrange the chicken in to your air fryer basket.
5. Air fry for 15 minutes or 'til the chicken is cooked through and slightly charred.
6. Warm pita bread in to your air fryer for the last 2 minutes.
7. Assemble the Greek-style chicken pita wraps with cut red onions, tomatoes, cucumbers, then your choice of sauce.
8. Enjoy these chicken wraps with a Mediterranean flair for a quick and delicious meal.

Per serving: Calories: 350kcal; Fat: 15g; Carbs: 30g; Protein: 25g

84. Lemon Rosemary Air-Fried Turkey Breast

Preparation time: 5 minutes
Cooking time: 25 minutes
Servings: 4
Ingredients:

- 1 turkey breast, boneless and skinless
- 2 tbsps. olive oil
- Zest and juice of 1 lemon
- 2 tsps. fresh rosemary, chopped
- 1 tsp. garlic powder
- Salt and pepper as required

Directions:

1. Warm up the air fryer to 375 °F.
2. In your bowl, mix olive oil, lemon zest, lemon juice, chopped fresh rosemary, garlic powder, salt, and pepper.
3. Coat the turkey breast with the lemon rosemary mixture.
4. Place turkey breast in to your air fryer basket.
5. Air fry for 25 minutes or 'til the turkey is cooked through then reaches an internal temp. of 165 °F.
6. Prior to cutting it, allow it to rest for a couple of precious minutes.
7. Serve this lemon rosemary air-fried turkey breast for a moist and flavorful main dish.
8. Enjoy the aromatic combination of lemon and rosemary with tender turkey.

Per serving: Calories: 300kcal; Fat: 15g; Carbs: 2g; Protein: 40g

85. Harissa Marinated Grilled Chicken Thighs

Preparation time: 15 minutes
Cooking time: 15 minutes
Servings: 4
Ingredients:

- 8 chicken thighs, bone-in and skin-on
- 2 tbsps. harissa paste
- 2 tbsps. olive oil
- 1 tsp. ground cumin
- 1 tsp. smoked paprika
- 1/2 tsp. ground coriander
- Salt and pepper as required
- Lemon wedges for presenting

Directions:

1. Warm up the air fryer to 400 °F.
2. In your bowl, mix harissa paste, olive oil, ground cumin, smoked paprika, ground coriander, salt, and pepper.
3. Coat chicken thighs with the harissa marinade.
4. Arrange the chicken thighs in to your air fryer basket.
5. Air fry for 15 minutes or 'til the chicken is cooked through then the skin is crispy.
6. Serve with your lemon wedges for a burst of citrusy flavor.
7. Enjoy these harissa marinated grilled chicken thighs for a spicy and aromatic dish.

Per serving: Calories: 400kcal; Fat: 30g; Carbs: 2g; Protein: 35g

86. Mediterranean Beef Kebabs with Tomato and Onion

Preparation time: 15 minutes
Cooking time: 15 minutes
Servings: 4
Ingredients:

- 1 lb. beef sirloin, cubes
- 2 tbsps. olive oil
- 1 tbsp. dried oregano
- 1 tsp. ground cumin
- 1 tsp. smoked paprika
- 1/2 tsp. garlic powder
- Salt and pepper as required
- Cherry tomatoes and red onion wedges for skewering
- Tzatziki sauce for presenting

Directions:

1. Warm up the air fryer to 400 °F.
2. In your bowl, mix olive oil, dried oregano, ground cumin, smoked paprika, garlic powder, salt, and pepper.
3. Coat beef cubes with the Mediterranean spice mixture.
4. Thread beef cubes, cherry tomatoes, and red onion wedges onto skewers.
5. Arrange the kebabs in to your air fryer basket.
6. Air fry for 15 minutes or 'til the beef is cooked to your desired doneness.
7. Serve these Mediterranean beef kebabs with a side of tzatziki sauce.
8. Enjoy the bold flavors of the Mediterranean in these succulent beef skewers.

Per serving: Calories: 400kcal; Fat: 30g; Carbs: 5g; Protein: 35g

87. Greek Chicken Souvlaki Skewers

Preparation time: 15 minutes
Cooking time: 10 minutes
Servings: 4
Ingredients:

- 1 lb. boneless, skinless chicken breasts, cubes
- 2 tbsps. olive oil
- 2 tbsps. Greek yogurt
- 1 tsp. dried oregano
- 1 tsp. dried thyme
- 1 tsp. smoked paprika
- 3 pieces garlic, crushed
- Salt and pepper as required
- Wooden skewers, soaked in water

Directions:

1. Warm up the air fryer to 375 °F.
2. In your bowl, mix olive oil, Greek yogurt, dried oregano, dried thyme, smoked paprika, crushed garlic, salt, and pepper.
3. Coat chicken cubes with the Greek marinade.
4. Thread marinated chicken onto the soaked wooden skewers.
5. Arrange the skewers in to your air fryer basket.
6. Air fry for 10 minutes or 'til the chicken is cooked through and slightly charred.
7. Serve these Greek chicken souvlaki skewers with your favorite tzatziki sauce.
8. Enjoy the authentic flavors of Greek cuisine in a quick and easy air-fried version.

Per serving: Calories: 250kcal; Fat: 10g; Carbs: 2g; Protein: 30g

88. Mediterranean Lamb and Chickpea Stew

Preparation time: 10 minutes
Cooking time: 30 minutes
Servings: 4
Ingredients:

- 1 lb. lamb stew meat
- 1 can (15 oz) chickpeas
- 1 onion, diced
- 2 carrots, cut
- 3 pieces garlic, crushed
- 1 can (14 oz) diced tomatoes
- 1 cup chicken broth
- 1 tsp. dried rosemary
- 1 tsp. dried thyme
- Salt and pepper as required

Directions:

1. Warm up the air fryer to 375 °F.
2. In to your air fryer basket, combine lamb stew meat, chickpeas, diced onion, cut carrots, crushed garlic, diced tomatoes, chicken broth, dried rosemary, dried thyme, salt, and pepper.
3. Mix everything well.
4. Air fry for 25-30 minutes, mixing irregularly, 'til the lamb is tender and the stew is flavorful.
5. Serve this Mediterranean lamb and chickpea stew with a side of crusty bread if desired.
6. Enjoy this hearty and comforting stew with the rich taste of lamb and chickpeas.

Per serving: Calories: 400kcal; Fat: 20g; Carbs: 30g; Protein: 25g

89. Air Fryer Lemon Garlic Herb Chicken Thighs

Preparation time: 10 minutes
Cooking time: 20 minutes
Servings: 4
Ingredients:

- 8 bone-in, skin-on chicken thighs
- 2 tbsps. olive oil
- Zest and juice of 1 lemon
- 3 pieces garlic, crushed
- 1 tbsp. fresh rosemary, chopped
- 1 tsp. dried thyme
- Salt and pepper as required

Directions:

1. Warm up the air fryer to 375 °F.
2. In your bowl, mix olive oil, lemon zest, lemon juice, crushed garlic, chopped fresh rosemary, dried thyme, salt, and pepper.
3. Coat chicken thighs with the lemon garlic herb mixture.
4. Arrange the chicken thighs in to your air fryer basket.
5. Air fry for 20 minutes or 'til the chicken is golden then reaches an internal temp. of 165 °F.
6. Serve these air fryer lemon garlic herb chicken thighs for a flavorful and juicy meal.
7. Enjoy the aromatic blend of lemon and herbs with perfectly cooked chicken.

Per serving: Calories: 400kcal; Fat: 30g; Carbs: 1g; Protein: 35g

90. Garlic and Herb Marinated Air Fryer Chicken Breasts

Preparation time: 10 minutes
Cooking time: 20 minutes
Servings: 4
Ingredients:

- 4 boneless, skinless chicken breasts
- 2 tbsps. olive oil
- 3 pieces garlic, crushed
- 1 tbsp. fresh parsley, chopped
- 1 tsp. dried thyme
- 1 tsp. dried rosemary
- Salt and pepper as required

Directions:

1. Warm up the air fryer to 375 °F.
2. In your bowl, mix olive oil, crushed garlic, chopped fresh parsley, dried thyme, dried rosemary, salt, and pepper.
3. Coat chicken breasts with the garlic and herb marinade.
4. Place chicken breasts in to your air fryer basket.
5. Air fry for 20 minutes or 'til the chicken is cooked through then has a golden crust.
6. Prior to cutting it, allow it to rest for a couple of precious minutes.
7. Serve these garlic and herb marinated air fryer chicken breasts for a fragrant and flavorful meal.
8. Enjoy the aromatic blend of garlic and herbs with tender chicken.

Per serving: Calories: 250kcal; Fat: 10g; Carbs: 1g; Protein: 35g

91. Moroccan-spiced Lamb Burgers

Preparation time: 15 minutes
Cooking time: 15 minutes
Servings: 4
Ingredients:

- 1 lb. ground lamb
- 1/4 cup breadcrumbs
- 1/4 cup dried apricots, finely chopped
- 1/4 cup almonds, chopped
- 2 tsps. ground cumin
- 1 tsp. ground coriander
- 1 tsp. smoked paprika
- Salt and pepper as required
- 4 whole wheat burger buns
- Yogurt sauce for topping
- Arugula and cut tomatoes for garnish

Directions:

1. Warm up the air fryer to 375 °F.
2. In your bowl, mix ground lamb, breadcrumbs, chopped dried apricots, chopped almonds, ground cumin, ground coriander, smoked paprika, salt, and pepper.
3. Form the mixture into burger patties.
4. Place lamb burgers in to your air fryer basket.
5. Air fry for 15 minutes or 'til the burgers are cooked through and have a slightly crispy exterior.
6. Toast the burger buns in to your air fryer for the last 2 minutes.
7. Serve the Moroccan-spiced lamb burgers on toasted buns with yogurt sauce, arugula, and cut tomatoes.
8. Enjoy these unique and flavorful lamb burgers with a Moroccan twist.

Per serving: Calories: 400kcal; Fat: 25g; Carbs: 20g; Protein: 30g

92. Greek Lamb Burger with Tzatziki Sauce

Preparation time: 15 minutes
Cooking time: 15 minutes
Servings: 4
Ingredients:

- 1 lb. ground lamb
- 1/4 cup breadcrumbs
- 1/4 cup red onion, finely chopped
- 2 pieces garlic, crushed
- 1 tsp. dried oregano
- 1 tsp. dried mint
- Salt and pepper as required
- 4 whole wheat burger buns
- Tzatziki sauce for topping
- Sliced cucumber, tomato, and red onion for garnish

Directions:

1. Warm up the air fryer to 375 °F.
2. In your bowl, mix ground lamb, breadcrumbs, chopped red onion, crushed garlic, dried oregano, dried mint, salt, and pepper.
3. Form the mixture into burger patties.
4. Place lamb burgers in to your air fryer basket.
5. Air fry for 15 minutes or 'til the burgers are cooked through and slightly charred.
6. Toast the burger buns in to your air fryer for the last 2 minutes.
7. Serve the Greek lamb burgers on toasted buns with tzatziki sauce and cut cucumber, tomato, and red onion.
8. Enjoy these flavorful Greek lamb burgers with a refreshing twist.

Per serving: Calories: 400kcal; Fat: 25g; Carbs: 20g; Protein: 30g

93. Baked Italian Herb Turkey Meatballs

Preparation time: 15 minutes
Cooking time: 15 minutes
Servings: 4
Ingredients:

- 1 lb. ground turkey
- 1/2 cup breadcrumbs
- 1/4 cup grated Parmesan cheese
- 1 tsp. dried oregano
- 1 tsp. dried basil
- 1/2 tsp. garlic powder
- 1/2 tsp. onion powder
- Salt and pepper as required
- Marinara sauce for presenting

Directions:

1. Warm up the air fryer to 375 °F.
2. In your bowl, mix ground turkey, breadcrumbs, grated Parmesan cheese, dried oregano, dried basil, garlic powder, onion powder, salt, and pepper.
3. Form the mixture into meatballs.
4. Place meatballs in to your air fryer basket.
5. Air fry for 15 minutes or 'til the meatballs are cooked through.
6. Serve these baked Italian herb turkey meatballs with marinara sauce.
7. Enjoy a lighter version of classic Italian meatballs with a hint of herbs.

Per serving: Calories: 250kcal; Fat: 15g; Carbs: 10g; Protein: 20g

94. Mediterranean Lamb Chops with Mint Chimichurri

Preparation time: 15 minutes
Cooking time: 12 minutes
Servings: 4
Ingredients:

- 8 lamb chops
- 2 tbsps. olive oil
- 3 pieces garlic, crushed
- 1 tbsp. fresh rosemary, chopped
- 1 tsp. dried oregano
- Salt and pepper as required

Mint Chimichurri Sauce:

- 1 cup fresh mint leaves
- 1 cup fresh parsley leaves
- 2 pieces garlic
- 1/4 cup red wine vinegar
- 1/2 cup olive oil
- Salt and pepper as required

Directions:

1. Warm up the air fryer to 400 °F.
2. In your bowl, mix olive oil, crushed garlic, chopped fresh rosemary, dried oregano, salt, and pepper.
3. Coat lamb chops with the herb mixture.
4. Arrange the lamb chops in to your air fryer basket.
5. Air fry for 12 minutes or 'til the lamb chops reach the desired level of doneness.
6. For the Mint Chimichurri Sauce, blend mint leaves, parsley leaves, garlic, red wine vinegar, and olive oil 'til smooth. Season using salt and pepper.
7. Serve the Mediterranean lamb chops with a drizzle of Mint Chimichurri Sauce.
8. Enjoy these succulent lamb chops with a refreshing minty twist.

Per serving: Calories: 400kcal; Fat: 30g; Carbs: 2g; Protein: 35g

95. Balsamic Glazed Air Fryer Chicken Quarters

Preparation time: 5 minutes
Cooking time: 25 minutes
Servings: 4
Ingredients:

- 4 chicken leg quarters
- 1/4 cup balsamic glaze
- 2 tbsps. olive oil
- 1 tsp. dried thyme
- 1 tsp. dried rosemary
- Salt and pepper as required

Directions:

1. Warm up the air fryer to 400 °F.
2. In your bowl, mix balsamic glaze, olive oil, dried thyme, dried rosemary, salt, and pepper.
3. Coat chicken leg quarters with the balsamic glaze mixture.
4. Place chicken quarters in to your air fryer basket.
5. Air fry for 25 minutes or 'til the chicken is cooked through and has a caramelized glaze.
6. When you are ready to serve it, wait a couple of minutes for it to rest.
7. Serve these balsamic glazed air fryer chicken quarters for a succulent and flavorful dish.
8. Enjoy the sweet and tangy taste of balsamic-glazed chicken.

Per serving: Calories: 450kcal; Fat: 30g; Carbs: 10g; Protein: 35g

96. Lemon Oregano Grilled Chicken Skewers

Preparation time: 15 minutes
Cooking time: 15 minutes
Servings: 4
Ingredients:

- 1.5 lbs. chicken breast, cubes
- 2 tbsps. olive oil
- Zest and juice of 1 lemon
- 2 tsps. dried oregano
- 1 tsp. garlic powder
- Salt and pepper as required
- Cherry tomatoes and red onion wedges for skewering

Directions:

1. Warm up the air fryer to 375 °F.
2. In your bowl, mix olive oil, lemon zest, lemon juice, dried oregano, garlic powder, salt, and pepper.
3. Coat chicken cubes with the lemon oregano mixture.
4. Thread chicken cubes, cherry tomatoes, and red onion wedges onto skewers.
5. Arrange the skewers in to your air fryer basket.
6. Air fry for 15 minutes or 'til the chicken is cooked through then has a golden color.
7. Serve these lemon oregano grilled chicken skewers with a side of tzatziki sauce if desired.
8. Enjoy the fresh and zesty flavors of Mediterranean-inspired grilled chicken.

Per serving: Calories: 350kcal; Fat: 15g; Carbs: 2g; Protein: 40g

97. Air-Fried Honey Mustard Glazed Chicken Drumettes

Preparation time: 10 minutes
Cooking time: 20 minutes
Servings: 4
Ingredients:

- 2 lbs. chicken drumettes
- 1/4 cup honey
- 2 tbsps. Dijon mustard
- 1 tbsp. soy sauce
- 1 tsp. garlic powder
- Salt and pepper as required
- Sesame seeds & chopped green onions

Directions:

1. Warm up the air fryer to 400 °F.
2. In your bowl, mix honey, Dijon mustard, soy sauce, garlic powder, salt, and pepper.
3. Coat chicken drumettes with the honey mustard glaze.
4. Arrange the drumettes in to your air fryer basket.
5. Air fry for 20 minutes or 'til the chicken is golden then cooked through.
6. Garnish using sesame seeds and chopped green onions prior to presenting.
7. Enjoy these air-fried honey mustard glazed chicken drumettes as a sweet and savory appetizer or main dish.

Per serving: Calories: 350kcal; Fat: 20g; Carbs: 15g; Protein: 25g

98. Crispy Italian Herb Pork Chops

Preparation time: 10 minutes
Cooking time: 20 minutes
Servings: 4
Ingredients:

- 4 bone-in pork chops
- 2 tbsps. olive oil
- 1 tbsp. dried Italian herbs (basil, oregano, thyme)
- 1 tsp. garlic powder
- Salt and pepper as required

Directions:

1. Warm up the air fryer to 400 °F.
2. In your bowl, mix olive oil, dried Italian herbs, garlic powder, salt, and pepper.
3. Coat pork chops with the Italian herb mixture.
4. Place pork chops in to your air fryer basket.
5. Air fry for 20 minutes or 'til the pork chops are cooked through and have a crispy exterior.
6. When you are ready to serve it, wait a couple of minutes for it to rest.
7. Serve these crispy Italian herb pork chops for a delightful and flavorful meal.
8. Enjoy the combination of aromatic herbs with perfectly cooked pork.

Per serving: Calories: 350kcal; Fat: 20g; Carbs: 1g; Protein: 40g

99. Greek-style Stuffed Cabbage Rolls with Ground Beef

Preparation time: 10 minutes
Cooking time: 20 minutes
Servings: 4
Ingredients:

- 1 head of cabbage
- 1 lb. ground beef
- 1 cup cooked rice
- 1/2 cup onion, finely chopped
- 2 pieces garlic, crushed
- 1 tsp. dried oregano
- 1 tsp. dried mint
- Salt and pepper as required
- 1 can (14 oz) crushed tomatoes
- 1/2 cup feta cheese, crumbled

Directions:

1. Warm up the air fryer to 375 °F.
2. Carefully peel off cabbage leaves and blanch them in boiling water for 2-3 minutes 'til softened.
3. In your bowl, mix ground beef, cooked rice, chopped onion, crushed garlic, dried oregano, dried mint, salt, and pepper.
4. Spoon the beef mixture onto the center of each cabbage leaf and roll them up, tucking in the sides.
5. Place cabbage rolls in to your air fryer basket.
6. Pour crushed tomatoes over the cabbage rolls and sprinkle crumbled feta on top.
7. Air fry for 20 minutes or 'til the cabbage is tender then the filling is cooked through.
8. Serve these Greek-style stuffed cabbage rolls with a drizzle of olive oil if desired.
9. Enjoy this unique twist on cabbage rolls with Mediterranean flavors.

Per serving: Calories: 400kcal; Fat: 20g; Carbs: 30g; Protein: 25g

100. Air-Fried Cajun Chicken Thighs

Preparation time: 10 minutes
Cooking time: 20 minutes
Servings: 4
Ingredients:

- 8 chicken thighs, bone-in and skin-on
- 2 tbsps. olive oil
- 1 tbsp. Cajun seasoning
- 1 tsp. garlic powder
- 1/2 tsp. smoked paprika
- Salt and pepper as required

Directions:

1. Warm up the air fryer to 400 °F.
2. In your bowl, mix olive oil, Cajun seasoning, garlic powder, smoked paprika, salt, and pepper.
3. Coat chicken thighs with the Cajun spice mixture.
4. Place chicken thighs in to your air fryer basket.
5. Air fry for 20 minutes or 'til the chicken is cooked through then the skin is crispy.
6. Serve these air-fried Cajun chicken thighs for a spicy and flavorful dish.
7. Enjoy the bold Cajun flavors with perfectly cooked chicken.

Per serving: Calories: 400kcal; Fat: 30g; Carbs: 2g; Protein: 35g

 # SIDES AND SALADS

101. Lemon and Olive Oil Roasted Potatoes

Preparation time: 10 minutes
Cooking time: 20 minutes
Servings: 4
Ingredients:

- 4 cups baby potatoes, divided
- 2 tbsps. olive oil
- Zest and juice of 1 lemon
- 2 pieces garlic, crushed
- 1 tsp. dried thyme
- Salt and pepper as required

Directions:

1. Warm up the air fryer to 400 °F.
2. In your bowl, toss baby potatoes using olive oil, lemon zest, lemon juice, crushed garlic, dried thyme, salt, and pepper.
3. Place seasoned potatoes in to your air fryer basket.
4. Air fry for 20 minutes or 'til the potatoes are golden and crispy.
5. Serve these lemon and olive oil roasted potatoes as a zesty and satisfying side dish.
6. Enjoy the bright flavors of lemon paired with perfectly roasted potatoes.

Per serving: Calories: 200kcal; Fat: 7g; Carbs: 30g; Protein: 3g

102. Roasted Eggplant and Tomato Caprese Salad

Preparation time: 15 minutes
Cooking time: 15 minutes
Servings: 4
Ingredients:

- 1 big eggplant, cut
- 1 cup cherry tomatoes, divided
- 1 cup fresh mozzarella, cut
- Fresh basil leaves
- 2 tbsps. balsamic glaze
- 2 tbsps. extra-virgin olive oil
- Salt and pepper as required

Directions:

1. Warm up the air fryer to 375 °F.
2. In your bowl, toss eggplant slices using olive oil, salt, and pepper.
3. Place eggplant slices in to your air fryer basket.
4. Air fry for 15 minutes or 'til the eggplant is tender and golden.
5. Arrange roasted eggplant, cherry tomatoes, and fresh mozzarella on a serving platter.
6. Drizzle with balsamic glaze.
7. Garnish with fresh basil leaves.
8. Serve this roasted eggplant and tomato Caprese salad for a delightful appetizer.

Per serving: Calories: 250kcal; Fat: 18g; Carbs: 15g; Protein: 10g

103. Air-Fried Falafel Salad with Tahini Dressing

Preparation time: 15 minutes
Cooking time: 10 minutes
Servings: 4
Ingredients:

- 1 can (15 oz) chickpeas
- 1/2 cup fresh parsley
- 1/4 cup chopped red onion
- 2 pieces garlic
- 1 tsp. ground cumin
- 1 tsp. ground coriander
- 1/2 tsp. baking soda
- Salt and pepper as required
- Olive oil cooking spray
- Mixed greens for the salad
- Cherry tomatoes, cucumber, and red onion for garnish

Tahini Dressing:

- 1/4 cup tahini
- 2 tbsps. lemon juice
- 2 tbsps. water
- 1 tbsp. olive oil
- Salt and pepper as required

Directions:

1. In the blending container that you have, combine chickpeas, fresh parsley, chopped red onion, garlic, ground cumin, ground coriander, baking soda, salt, and pepper.
2. Pulse 'til the mixture forms a coarse paste.
3. Form the mixture into small falafel balls.
4. Warm up the air fryer to 375 °F.
5. Spray the falafel balls using olive oil cooking spray.
6. Place falafel balls in to your air fryer basket.
7. Air fry for 10 minutes or 'til the falafel is golden and crispy.
8. To prepare the dressing, combine the following components in a small bowl: salt, tahini, lemon juice, water, olive oil, and pepper. Whisk until well combined.
9. Arrange mixed greens on your plate, top with air-fried falafel, and garnish with cherry tomatoes, cucumber, and red onion.
10. Drizzle the tahini dressing over the salad.
11. Serve this air-fried falafel salad for a delicious and healthy meal.
12. Enjoy the crunchy falafel paired with the creamy tahini dressing.

Per serving: Calories: 300kcal; Fat: 18g; Carbs: 25g; Protein: 10g

104. Air Fryer Stuffed Grape Leaves (Dolma) with Rice

Preparation time: 20 minutes
Cooking time: 10 minutes
Servings: 4
Ingredients:

- 1 jar grape leaves
- 1 cup cooked rice
- 1/2 cup pine nuts, toasted
- 1/4 cup fresh dill, chopped
- 1/4 cup fresh mint, chopped
- 1/4 cup extra-virgin olive oil
- Juice of 1 lemon
- Salt and pepper as required

Directions:

1. In your bowl, combine cooked rice, toasted pine nuts, chopped fresh dill, chopped fresh mint, extra-virgin olive oil, lemon juice, salt, and pepper.
2. Position your grape leaf so that the shiny side is facing down on a level surface.
3. Spoon a small amount of the rice mixture onto the middle of the grape leaf.
4. Fold sides of the grape leaf over your filling and roll it up tightly.
5. Warm up the air fryer to 375 °F.
6. Put stuffed grape leaves in to your air fryer basket.
7. Air fry for 10 minutes or 'til the grape leaves are heated through.
8. Serve these air-fried stuffed grape leaves with rice as a delightful appetizer or side.
9. Enjoy the savory and herb-infused flavors of this classic Mediterranean dish.

Per serving: Calories: 250kcal; Fat: 15g; Carbs: 25g; Protein: 5g

105. Air Fryer Garlic Herb Roasted Vegetables

Preparation time: 10 minutes
Cooking time: 15 minutes
Servings: 4
Ingredients:

- 2 cups baby potatoes, divided
- 1 cup baby carrots
- 1 cup broccoli florets
- 1 cup cauliflower florets
- 2 tbsps. olive oil
- 2 pieces garlic, crushed
- 1 tsp. dried thyme
- 1 tsp. dried rosemary
- Salt and pepper as required

Directions:

1. Warm up the air fryer to 375 °F.
2. In your big bowl, toss baby potatoes, baby carrots, broccoli florets, and cauliflower florets using olive oil, crushed garlic, dried thyme, dried rosemary, salt, and pepper.
3. Place seasoned vegetables in to your air fryer basket.
4. Air fry for 15 minutes or 'til the vegetables are tender and golden.
5. Serve these air-fried garlic herb roasted vegetables as a flavorful side dish.
6. Enjoy the crispy texture and aromatic herbs of these roasted veggies.

Per serving: Calories: 150kcal; Fat: 7g; Carbs: 20g; Protein: 3g

106. Lemon Garlic Roasted Brussels Sprouts

Preparation time: 10 minutes
Cooking time: 15 minutes
Servings: 4
Ingredients:

- 1 lb. Brussels sprouts, clipped and divided
- 2 tbsps. olive oil
- 3 pieces garlic, crushed
- Zest of 1 lemon
- Juice of 1 lemon
- Salt and pepper as required

Directions:

1. Warm up the air fryer to 375 °F.
2. In your bowl, toss Brussels sprouts using olive oil, crushed garlic, lemon zest, lemon juice, salt, and pepper.
3. Put seasoned Brussels sprouts in to your air fryer basket.
4. Air fry for 15 minutes or 'til the Brussels sprouts are golden and crispy.
5. Serve these lemon garlic roasted Brussels sprouts as a flavorful side dish.
6. Enjoy the zesty and aromatic combination of lemon and garlic.

Per serving: Calories: 150kcal; Fat: 8g; Carbs: 20g; Protein: 5g

107. Air-Fried Zucchini Fritters with Tzatziki

Preparation time: 15 minutes
Cooking time: 10 minutes
Servings: 4
Ingredients:

- 2 medium zucchinis, grated and excess moisture squeezed out
- 1/2 cup breadcrumbs
- 1/4 cup grated Parmesan cheese
- 1 egg
- 1 tsp. dried dill
- Salt and pepper as required
- Olive oil cooking spray
- Tzatziki sauce for dipping

Directions:

1. In your bowl, combine grated zucchini, breadcrumbs, grated Parmesan cheese, egg, dried dill, salt, and pepper.
2. Mix until everything is thoroughly incorporated.
3. Form the mixture into small fritters.
4. Warm up the air fryer to 375 °F.
5. Spray the air fryer basket using olive oil cooking spray.
6. Place zucchini fritters in to your air fryer basket.
7. Air fry for 10 minutes or 'til the fritters are golden and crispy.
8. Serve these air-fried zucchini fritters with tzatziki sauce for dipping.
9. Enjoy the crunchy exterior and tender interior of these flavorful fritters.

Per serving: Calories: 150kcal; Fat: 8g; Carbs: 15g; Protein: 6g

108. Grilled Halloumi and Watermelon Salad

Preparation time: 15 minutes
Cooking time: 5 minutes
Servings: 4
Ingredients:

- 1/2 watermelon, cubes
- 8 oz. halloumi cheese, cut
- 2 cups arugula
- 1/4 cup fresh mint leaves
- 2 tbsps. extra-virgin olive oil
- 1 tbsp. balsamic glaze
- Salt and pepper as required

Directions:

1. Warm up the air fryer to 375 °F.
2. Grill halloumi slices in to your air fryer for 3-5 minutes or 'til golden.
3. In your big bowl, combine watermelon cubes, grilled halloumi, arugula, and fresh mint leaves.
4. Drizzle using extra-virgin olive oil and balsamic glaze.
5. Toss the salad 'til well combined.
6. Serve this grilled halloumi and watermelon salad for a refreshing and savory dish.

Per serving: Calories: 300kcal; Fat: 20g; Carbs: 25g; Protein: 10g

109. Air Fryer Greek-style Fish Tacos

Preparation time: 15 minutes
Cooking time: 10 minutes
Servings: 4
Ingredients:

- 1 lb. white fish fillets (e.g., cod or tilapia)
- 1 tbsp. olive oil
- 1 tsp. dried oregano
- 1 tsp. dried thyme
- 1/2 tsp. garlic powder
- Salt and pepper as required
- 8 small corn tortillas
- Tzatziki sauce for topping
- Sliced cucumber and cherry tomatoes for garnish

Directions:

1. Warm up the air fryer to 375 °F.
2. In your bowl, mix olive oil, dried oregano, dried thyme, garlic powder, salt, and pepper.
3. Coat fish fillets with the herb mixture.
4. Arrange the fillets in to your air fryer basket.
5. Air fry for 10 minutes or 'til the fish is cooked through and flakes easily.
6. Heat corn tortillas and assemble tacos with tzatziki sauce, cut cucumber, and cherry tomatoes.
7. Serve these air fryer Greek-style fish tacos for a delightful and Mediterranean-inspired meal.

Per serving: Calories: 300kcal; Fat: 10g; Carbs: 25g; Protein: 20g

110. Greek-style Grilled Octopus Salad

Preparation time: 10 minutes
Cooking time: 15 minutes
Servings: 4
Ingredients:

- 1 lb. octopus, cleaned and tentacles separated
- 2 tbsps. olive oil
- 2 pieces garlic, crushed
- 1 tsp. dried oregano
- Juice of 1 lemon
- Salt and pepper as required
- Cherry tomatoes, cucumber, red onion, and feta for the salad

Directions:

1. Warm up the air fryer to 375 °F.
2. In your bowl, toss octopus tentacles using olive oil, crushed garlic, dried oregano, lemon juice, salt, and pepper.
3. Place octopus in to your air fryer basket.
4. Air fry for 15 minutes or 'til the octopus is tender and slightly charred.
5. Serve the grilled octopus over a salad of cherry tomatoes, cucumber, red onion, and feta.
6. Enjoy this Mediterranean-inspired grilled octopus salad.

Per serving: Calories: 180kcal; Fat: 8g; Carbs: 8g; Protein: 20g

111. Air-Fried Stuffed Mushrooms with Spinach and Feta

Preparation time: 15 minutes
Cooking time: 10 minutes
Servings: 4
Ingredients:

- 16 big mushrooms, stems taken out and reserved
- 1 cup fresh spinach, chopped
- 1/2 cup feta cheese, crumbled
- 2 pieces garlic, crushed
- 2 tbsps. breadcrumbs
- 2 tbsps. extra-virgin olive oil
- 1 tbsp. fresh parsley, chopped
- Salt and pepper as required

Directions:

1. Warm up the air fryer to 375 °F.
2. Chop the reserved mushroom stems.
3. In your skillet, sauté chopped mushroom stems, chopped fresh spinach, crushed garlic, breadcrumbs, and extra-virgin olive oil 'til the spinach wilts and the mixture is well combined.
4. Take it off the fire and allow it to cool down a little bit.
5. In your bowl, mix the sautéed mixture with crumbled feta, chopped fresh parsley, salt, and pepper.
6. Stuff each mushroom cap with using spinach and feta mixture.
7. Place stuffed mushrooms in to your air fryer basket.
8. Air fry for 10 minutes or 'til the mushrooms are tender then the filling is golden.
9. Serve these air-fried stuffed mushrooms as a delightful appetizer or side.
10. Enjoy the savory combination of spinach and feta in each bite.

Per serving: Calories: 150kcal; Fat: 10g; Carbs: 10g; Protein: 5g

112. Lemon Herb Air-Fried Sorghum Salad

Preparation time: 10 minutes
Cooking time: 15 minutes
Servings: 3
Ingredients:

- 1 cup sorghum, cooked
- Zest and juice of 1 lemon
- 2 tbsps. chopped fresh herbs (e.g., mint or parsley)
- 1 tbsp. olive oil
- 1/4 cup diced cucumber
- 1/4 cup cherry tomatoes, divided
- Salt and pepper as required

Directions:

1. Warm up the air fryer to 375 °F.
2. In your bowl, mix together cooked sorghum, lemon zest, lemon juice, chopped herbs, olive oil, diced cucumber, cherry tomatoes, salt, and pepper.
3. Transfer the sorghum mixture to the air fryer basket.
4. Air fry for 15 minutes or 'til the salad is warmed through.

Per serving: Calories: 180kcal; Fat: 6g; Carbs: 27g; Protein: 4g

113. Air-Fried Lemon Herb Fish Tacos

Preparation time: 15 minutes
Cooking time: 10 minutes
Servings: 4
Ingredients:

- 1 lb. white fish fillets (e.g., cod or tilapia)
- 2 tbsps. olive oil
- Zest and juice of 1 lemon
- 1 tsp. dried oregano
- 1 tsp. cumin
- 1/2 tsp. garlic powder
- Salt and pepper as required
- 8 small corn tortillas
- Shredded cabbage, diced tomatoes, and cilantro for topping
- Lime wedges for presenting

Directions:

1. Warm up the air fryer to 375 °F.
2. In your bowl, mix olive oil, lemon zest, lemon juice, dried oregano, cumin, garlic powder, salt, and pepper.
3. Coat fish fillets with the lemon herb mixture.
4. Arrange the fillets in to your air fryer basket.
5. Air fry for 10 minutes or 'til the fish is cooked through and flakes easily.
6. Heat corn tortillas and assemble tacos with shredded cabbage, diced tomatoes, and cilantro.
7. Serve with your lime wedges for a burst of citrus flavor.
8. Enjoy these air-fried lemon herb fish tacos for a delightful meal.

Per serving: Calories: 250kcal; Fat: 10g; Carbs: 30g; Protein: 15g

114. Crispy Calamari Rings with Tzatziki Dip

Preparation time: 15 minutes
Cooking time: 10 minutes
Servings: 4
Ingredients:

- 1 lb. calamari rings, cleaned and thawed if frozen
- 1 cup buttermilk
- 1 cup all-purpose flour
- 1 tsp. smoked paprika
- 1/2 tsp. garlic powder
- Salt and pepper as required
- Olive oil spray
- Tzatziki dip for presenting

Directions:

1. Place calamari rings in a bowl then pour buttermilk over them. Let them soak for 15 minutes.
2. In your separate bowl, combine all-purpose flour, smoked paprika, garlic powder, salt, and pepper.
3. Drain the buttermilk from the calamari then toss them in the flour mixture to coat evenly.
4. Warm up the air fryer to 375 °F.
5. Arrange the coated calamari rings in a single layer in to your air fryer basket.
6. Mildly spray the calamari using olive oil.
7. Air fry for 10 minutes or 'til the calamari are golden and crispy.
8. Serve the crispy calamari rings with tzatziki dip.
9. Enjoy this delightful and crunchy seafood snack.

Per serving: Calories: 250kcal; Fat: 8g; Carbs: 30g; Protein: 15g

115. Air Fryer Spanakopita Bites

Preparation time: 15 minutes
Cooking time: 10 minutes
Servings: 4
Ingredients:

- 1 package (10 oz) frozen chopped spinach
- 1/2 cup feta cheese, crumbled
- 1/4 cup ricotta cheese
- 1/4 cup grated Parmesan cheese
- 1/4 cup fresh dill, chopped
- 2 pieces garlic, crushed
- 1 package (25 count) mini phyllo shells
- Olive oil cooking spray

Directions:

1. In your bowl, combine thawed and drained chopped spinach, crumbled feta cheese, ricotta cheese, grated Parmesan cheese, chopped fresh dill, and crushed garlic.
2. Warm up the air fryer to 375 °F.
3. Spoon the spinach and cheese mixture into mini phyllo shells.
4. Place filled phyllo shells in to your air fryer basket.
5. Spray the tops using olive oil cooking spray.
6. Air fry for 10 minutes or 'til the spanakopita bites are golden and crispy.
7. Serve these air-fried spanakopita bites as a delightful appetizer or snack.
8. Enjoy the flaky layers filled with spinach and cheesy goodness.

Per serving: Calories: 180kcal; Fat: 10g; Carbs: 15g; Protein: 8g

116. Baked Feta Cheese with Tomatoes and Herbs

Preparation time: 10 minutes
Cooking time: 15 minutes
Servings: 4
Ingredients:

- 1 block (8 oz) feta cheese
- 1 cup cherry tomatoes, divided
- 2 tbsps. fresh basil, chopped
- 2 tbsps. fresh oregano, chopped
- 2 tbsps. extra-virgin olive oil
- 1 tbsp. balsamic glaze
- Salt and pepper as required

Directions:

1. Warm up the air fryer to 375 °F.
2. Place block of feta cheese in the middle of an oven-safe dish.
3. Arrange divided cherry tomatoes around the feta cheese.
4. Sprinkle chopped fresh basil and oregano over the tomatoes and feta.
5. Drizzle using extra-virgin olive oil and balsamic glaze.
6. Season using salt and pepper as required.
7. Air fry for 15 minutes or 'til the feta is soft and tomatoes are roasted.
8. Serve this baked feta cheese with tomatoes and herbs as a warm and savory appetizer.
9. Enjoy the gooey and flavorful feta paired with the burst of roasted tomatoes.

Per serving: Calories: 200kcal; Fat: 15g; Carbs: 10g; Protein: 8g

117. Air Fryer Greek Potatoes with Oregano and Lemon Zest

Preparation time: 10 minutes
Cooking time: 20 minutes
Servings: 4
Ingredients:

- 4 big potatoes, cut into wedges
- 2 tbsps. extra-virgin olive oil
- 1 tsp. dried oregano
- Zest of 1 lemon
- Salt and pepper as required

Directions:

1. Warm up the air fryer to 375 °F.
2. In your bowl, toss potato wedges with extra-virgin olive oil, dried oregano, lemon zest, salt, and pepper.
3. Place seasoned potato wedges in to your air fryer basket.
4. Air fry for 20 minutes or 'til the potatoes are golden and crispy.
5. Transfer the air-fried Greek potatoes to a serving platter.
6. Serve these potatoes with oregano and lemon zest as a delicious and aromatic side.
7. Enjoy the combination of crispy exteriors and tender interiors with Greek-inspired flavors.

Per serving: Calories: 180kcal; Fat: 6g; Carbs: 30g; Protein: 3g

118. Greek-style Roasted Vegetable Platter

Preparation time: 15 minutes
Cooking time: 15 minutes
Servings: 4
Ingredients:

- 1 zucchini, cut
- 1 yellow bell pepper, cut
- 1 red onion, cut
- 1 cup cherry tomatoes
- 1/2 cup Kalamata olives, pitted
- 2 tbsps. extra-virgin olive oil
- 1 tsp. dried oregano
- Salt and pepper as required

Directions:

1. Warm up the air fryer to 375 °F.
2. In your big bowl, toss cut zucchini, yellow bell pepper, red onion, cherry tomatoes, and Kalamata olives with extra-virgin olive oil, dried oregano, salt, and pepper.
3. Arrange the seasoned vegetables in to your air fryer basket.
4. Fry the vegetables in an air fryer for 15 minutes, or until they are soft and have a mild caramelization.
5. Serve this Greek-style roasted vegetable platter as a colorful and flavorful side.
6. Enjoy the combination of roasted veggies with the richness of Kalamata olives.

Per serving: Calories: 150kcal; Fat: 10g; Carbs: 15g; Protein: 2g

119. Air-Fried Chicken Shawarma Bowls

Preparation time: 10 minutes
Cooking time: 20 minutes
Servings: 4
Ingredients:

- 1 lb. chicken thighs, that is boneless and skinless, cut
- 2 tbsps. olive oil
- 2 tsps. ground cumin
- 1 tsp. ground coriander
- 1 tsp. smoked paprika
- 1 tsp. ground turmeric
- 1 tsp. ground cinnamon
- Salt and pepper as required
- Cooked quinoa or rice for presenting
- Toppings: Hummus, diced cucumber, cherry tomatoes, red onion, and parsley

Directions:

1. Warm up the air fryer to 375 °F.
2. In your bowl, mix olive oil, ground cumin, ground coriander, smoked paprika, ground turmeric, ground cinnamon, salt, and pepper.
3. Coat chicken slices with the shawarma spice mixture.
4. Arrange the chicken in to your air fryer basket.
5. Air fry for 20 minutes or 'til the chicken is cooked through and has a slightly crispy exterior.
6. While chicken is cooking, prepare the quinoa or rice and the toppings.
7. Serve the air-fried chicken shawarma over cooked quinoa or rice, topped with hummus, diced cucumber, cherry tomatoes, red onion, and parsley.
8. Enjoy these delectable chicken shawarma bowls for a quick and satisfying meal.

Per serving: Calories: 400kcal; Fat: 20g; Carbs: 30g; Protein: 25g

120. Grilled Asparagus with Lemon and Parmesan

Preparation time: 10 minutes
Cooking time: 10 minutes
Servings: 4
Ingredients:

- 1 bunch asparagus, tough ends clipped
- 2 tbsps. extra-virgin olive oil
- Zest of 1 lemon
- 2 tbsps. freshly grated Parmesan cheese
- Salt and pepper as required

Directions:

1. Warm up the air fryer to 375 °F.
2. Toss asparagus with extra-virgin olive oil, lemon zest, salt, and pepper in a bowl.
3. Place seasoned asparagus in to your air fryer basket.
4. Air fry for 10 minutes or 'til the asparagus is tender-crisp.
5. Transfer grilled asparagus to a serving plate.
6. Sprinkle freshly grated Parmesan cheese over your asparagus.
7. Serve this grilled asparagus with lemon and Parmesan as a simple and elegant side.
8. Enjoy the bright and citrusy flavors combined with the nuttiness of Parmesan.

Per serving: Calories: 80kcal; Fat: 6g; Carbs: 5g; Protein: 3g

 # GRAINS AND LEGUMES

121. Air Fryer Brown Rice Pilaf with Mixed Herbs

Preparation time: 10 minutes
Cooking time: 15 minutes
Servings: 4
Ingredients:

- 1 cup brown rice
- 2 cups vegetable broth
- 1/4 cup fresh parsley, chopped
- 1/4 cup fresh cilantro, chopped
- 1/4 cup fresh mint, chopped
- 1/4 cup almonds, cut and toasted
- 2 tbsps. olive oil
- Salt and pepper as required

Directions:

1. In your saucepan, bring vegetable broth to a boil. Stir in brown rice then cook according to package instructions.
2. Once rice is cooked, fluff it with a fork.
3. In your bowl, toss the cooked brown rice with chopped fresh parsley, chopped fresh cilantro, chopped fresh mint, toasted cut almonds, olive oil, salt, and pepper.
4. Transfer the rice mixture to the air fryer basket.
5. Warm up the air fryer to 375 °F.
6. Air fry the brown rice pilaf for 10-15 minutes or 'til the edges are crispy.
7. Serve this air-fried brown rice pilaf with mixed herbs as a flavorful and textured side dish.
8. Enjoy the aromatic blend of herbs and the crunch of toasted almonds.

Per serving: Calories: 280kcal; Fat: 12g; Carbs: 35g; Protein: 6g

122. Air-Fried Harissa Chickpeas

Preparation time: 5 minutes
Cooking time: 15 minutes
Servings: 4
Ingredients:

- 2 cans (15 oz each) chickpeas
- 2 tbsps. harissa paste
- 1 tbsp. olive oil
- 1 tsp. ground cumin
- 1/2 tsp. smoked paprika
- Salt and pepper as required

Directions:

1. Warm up the air fryer to 400 °F.
2. In your bowl, toss chickpeas with salt, harissa paste, olive oil, cumin, smoked paprika, and pepper.
3. Transfer the chickpea mixture to the air fryer basket.
4. Air fry for 15 minutes or 'til the chickpeas are crispy and slightly charred.

Per serving: Calories: 230kcal; Fat: 8g; Carbs: 30g; Protein: 9g

123. Mediterranean Couscous with Roasted Vegetables

Preparation time: 15 minutes
Cooking time: 15 minutes
Servings: 4
Ingredients:

- 1 cup couscous
- 1 1/2 cups vegetable broth
- 1 zucchini, diced
- 1 red bell pepper, diced
- 1 yellow bell pepper, diced
- 1 red onion, cut
- 2 tbsps. extra-virgin olive oil
- 1 tsp. dried oregano
- 1 tsp. ground cumin
- Salt and pepper as required
- 1/4 cup feta cheese, crumbled (garnish)
- Fresh parsley, chopped (for garnish)

Directions:

1. Warm up the air fryer to 375 °F.
2. In your bowl, toss diced zucchini, diced red and yellow bell peppers, and cut red onion with extra-virgin olive oil, dried oregano, ground cumin, salt, and pepper.
3. Disperse the seasoned vegetables in to your air fryer basket.
4. Air fry for 15 minutes or 'til the vegetables are roasted and tender.
5. In your separate saucepan, bring vegetable broth to a boil. Stir in couscous, cover, and wait for it to relax for 5 minutes.
6. Fluff couscous using a fork and transfer it to a serving platter.
7. Top the couscous with the air-fried Mediterranean roasted vegetables.
8. Garnish with crumbled feta cheese and chopped fresh parsley.
9. Serve this Mediterranean couscous with roasted vegetables as a vibrant and flavorful dish.
10. Enjoy the combination of fluffy couscous and colorful roasted veggies.

Per serving: Calories: 300kcal; Fat: 10g; Carbs: 45g; Protein: 8g

124. Lentil and Vegetable Stuffed Grape Leaves (Dolma)

Preparation time: 10 minutes
Cooking time: 20 minutes
Servings: 4
Ingredients:

- 1 cup brown lentils, cooked
- 1 cup cooked white rice
- 1/2 cup red onion, finely chopped
- 1/4 cup fresh dill, chopped
- 1/4 cup fresh mint, chopped
- 1/4 cup pine nuts
- 1/4 cup golden raisins
- 1/4 cup extra-virgin olive oil
- Juice of 1 lemon
- Salt and pepper as required
- Grape leaves, preserved in brine (for stuffing)

Directions:

1. In your bowl, combine cooked brown lentils, cooked white rice, chopped red onion, chopped fresh dill, chopped fresh mint, pine nuts, golden raisins, olive oil, lemon juice, salt, and pepper.
2. Rinse grape leaves under cold water to remove excess brine.
3. Put a grape leaf flat on a work surface, vein side up.
4. Spoon a small amount of the lentil and rice mixture onto the center of the leaf.
5. Fold sides of the grape leaf over your filling and roll from the bottom to the top to form a stuffed grape leaf.
6. Repeat the process 'til all the filling is used.
7. Place stuffed grape leaves in to your air fryer basket.
8. Warm up the air fryer to 375 °F.
9. Air fry the stuffed grape leaves for 15-20 minutes or 'til they are heated through and the leaves are slightly crispy.
10. Serve these lentil and vegetable stuffed grape leaves as a delightful appetizer or side dish.
11. Enjoy the combination of tender grape leaves and a flavorful, herb-infused filling.

Per serving: Calories: 280kcal; Fat: 14g; Carbs: 35g; Protein: 8g

125. Air-Fried Bulgur Pilaf with Pine Nuts

Preparation time: 15 minutes
Cooking time: 15 minutes
Servings: 4
Ingredients:

- 1 cup coarse bulgur
- 2 cups vegetable broth
- 1/4 cup pine nuts
- 1 onion, finely chopped
- 2 tbsps. olive oil
- 1 tsp. ground cumin
- 1 tsp. ground coriander
- Salt and pepper as required
- Fresh mint, chopped (for garnish)

Directions:

1. In your saucepan, combine coarse bulgur and vegetable broth. Boil, decrease temp., cover, then simmer for 15 minutes or 'til bulgur is cooked.
2. While the bulgur is cooking, toast pine nuts in to your air fryer at 375 °F for 3-4 minutes or 'til golden brown.
3. In your skillet, sauté finely chopped onion in olive oil 'til softened.
4. Include cooked bulgur to the skillet and stir in ground cumin, ground coriander, salt, and pepper.
5. Transfer the bulgur mixture to a serving dish.
6. Top using toasted pine nuts and chopped fresh mint.
7. Serve this air-fried bulgur pilaf as a flavorful and nutty side dish.
8. Enjoy the combination of fluffy bulgur and crunchy pine nuts.

Per serving: Calories: 250kcal; Fat: 10g; Carbs: 35g; Protein: 6g

126. Mushroom and Spinach Air Fryer Risotto

Preparation time: 10 minutes
Cooking time: 20 minutes
Servings: 3
Ingredients:

- 1 cup Arborio rice
- 2 cups vegetable broth
- 1/2 cup diced mushrooms
- 1 cup fresh spinach leaves
- 1/4 cup grated Parmesan cheese
- 2 tbsps. olive oil
- 1/2 cup diced onion
- 2 pieces garlic, crushed
- Salt and pepper as required

Directions:

1. Warm up the air fryer to 375 °F.
2. In a pan, sauté diced onion and crushed garlic in olive oil until softened.
3. Include Arborio rice and cook, stirring, for 2-3 minutes.
4. Pour in vegetable broth, diced mushrooms, and fresh spinach. Stir well.
5. Transfer mixture to the air fryer basket.
6. Air fry for 20 minutes, stirring halfway through, or until the rice is creamy and cooked through.
7. Stir in your grated Parmesan cheese and season with salt and pepper.
8. Serve warm as a delicious and hassle-free risotto.

Per serving: Calories: 380kcal; Fat: 14g; Carbs: 52g; Protein: 10g

127. Air Fryer Mujadara (Lentils and Rice)

Preparation time: 10 minutes
Cooking time: 20 minutes
Servings: 4
Ingredients:

- 1 cup brown lentils, washed
- 1 cup basmati rice, washed
- 2 onions, cut
- 4 cups vegetable broth
- 2 tsps. ground cumin
- 1 tsp. ground coriander
- 1/2 tsp. ground cinnamon
- 2 tbsps. olive oil
- Salt and pepper as required
- Fresh parsley, chopped (for garnish)

Directions:

1. Warm up the air fryer to 375 °F.
2. In your pot, combine brown lentils, basmati rice, cut onions, vegetable broth, ground cumin, ground coriander, ground cinnamon, olive oil, salt, and pepper.
3. Boil mixture, then decrease temp. and simmer for 20 minutes or 'til the lentils and rice are cooked.
4. While the mujadara is cooking, spread the cut onions in to your air fryer basket.
5. Air fry the onions for 10-12 minutes or 'til they are crispy and golden brown.
6. Serve the mujadara in bowls, topped with crispy air-fried onions.
7. Garnish with chopped fresh parsley.
8. Enjoy this air-fried mujadara as a hearty and flavorful dish.
9. Experience the rich blend of lentils, rice, and aromatic spices.

Per serving: Calories: 400kcal; Fat: 8g; Carbs: 70g; Protein: 15g

128. Air-Fried Quinoa and Black Bean Patties

Preparation time: 15 minutes
Cooking time: 15 minutes
Servings: 4
Ingredients:

- 1 cup cooked quinoa
- 1 can (15 oz) black beans
- 1/2 cup breadcrumbs
- 1/4 cup red onion, finely chopped
- 2 pieces garlic, crushed
- 1 tsp. ground cumin
- 1 tsp. chili powder
- Salt and pepper as required
- 2 tbsps. olive oil
- Avocado slices (for presenting)

Directions:

1. In the blending container that you have, combine cooked quinoa, black beans, breadcrumbs, chopped red onion, crushed garlic, ground cumin, chili powder, salt, and pepper.
2. Pulse 'til the mixture forms a cohesive texture.
3. Form the mixture into patties.
4. Warm up the air fryer to 375 °F.
5. Brush the quinoa and black bean patties using olive oil.
6. Air fry the patties for 15 minutes or 'til golden brown and crispy.
7. Serve these air-fried quinoa and black bean patties with slices of avocado.
8. Enjoy the crunchy exterior and flavorful interior of these plant-based patties.

Per serving: Calories: 300kcal; Fat: 10g; Carbs: 45g; Protein: 10g

129. Baked Eggplant and Lentil Stuffed Peppers

Preparation time: 10 minutes
Cooking time: 20 minutes
Servings: 4
Ingredients:

- 1 cup freekeh, washed and drained
- 2 cups vegetable broth
- 1 tbsp. olive oil
- 1 onion, finely chopped
- 2 pieces garlic, crushed
- 1 cup cherry tomatoes, divided
- 1/2 cup chopped fresh parsley
- 1/4 cup chopped fresh mint
- Zest and juice of 1 lemon
- Salt and pepper as required
- 1/4 cup crumbled feta cheese (garnish)

Directions:

1. In your medium saucepan, heat olive oil at middling temp.
2. Include chopped onion and sauté 'til softened, around 3-4 minutes.
3. Stir in crushed garlic then cook for an extra 1-2 minutes 'til fragrant.
4. Include washed freekeh to the saucepan and toast for 2-3 minutes, mixing irregularly.
5. Pour in vegetable broth, boil, then decrease temp. to low, cover, and simmer for 15-20 minutes or 'til freekeh is tender and liquid is absorbed.
6. Take out from heat then let it sit, covered, for 5 minutes.
7. Fluff the freekeh with a fork and transfer to a serving dish.
8. Gently fold in cherry tomatoes, chopped parsley, chopped mint, lemon zest, and lemon juice.
9. Season using salt and pepper as required and garnish with crumbled feta if desired.
10. Serve warm as a flavorful side dish or a light main course.

Per serving: Calories: 230 kcal; Fat: 6g; Carbs: 38g; Protein: 8g

130. Quinoa and Chickpea Stuffed Bell Peppers

Preparation time: 10 minutes
Cooking time: 20 minutes
Servings: 4
Ingredients:

- 1 cup quinoa, cooked
- 1 can (15 oz) chickpeas
- 4 bell peppers, divided and seeds taken out
- 1 cup cherry tomatoes, divided
- 1/4 cup red onion, finely chopped
- 1/4 cup black olives, cut
- 1/4 cup feta cheese, crumbled
- 2 tbsps. fresh parsley, chopped
- 1 tsp. dried oregano
- Salt and pepper as required
- 2 tbsps. olive oil

Directions:

1. In your bowl, combine cooked quinoa, drained chickpeas, cherry tomatoes, chopped red onion, cut black olives, crumbled feta cheese, chopped fresh parsley, dried oregano, salt, and pepper.
2. Warm up the air fryer to 375 °F.
3. Fill each bell pepper half with using quinoa and chickpea mixture.
4. Drizzle olive oil over the stuffed bell peppers.
5. Air fry the stuffed bell peppers for 15-20 minutes or 'til the peppers are tender.
6. Serve these quinoa and chickpea stuffed bell peppers as a wholesome and flavorful main course.
7. Enjoy the Mediterranean-inspired combination of quinoa, chickpeas, and veggies.

Per serving: Calories: 350kcal; Fat: 15g; Carbs: 45g; Protein: 12g

131. Air Fryer Greek Chickpea Patties

Preparation time: 15 minutes
Cooking time: 15 minutes
Servings: 4
Ingredients:

- 2 cans (15 oz each) chickpeas
- 1/2 cup breadcrumbs
- 1/4 cup red onion, finely chopped
- 2 pieces garlic, crushed
- 1 tsp. ground cumin
- 1 tsp. dried oregano
- Salt and pepper as required
- 2 tbsps. olive oil

Directions:

1. In the blending container that you have, combine chickpeas, breadcrumbs, chopped red onion, crushed garlic, ground cumin, dried oregano, salt, and pepper.
2. Pulse 'til the mixture forms a coarse texture.
3. Form the mixture into patties.
4. Warm up the air fryer to 375 °F.
5. Brush the chickpea patties using olive oil.
6. Air fry the patties for 15 minutes or 'til golden brown and crispy.
7. Serve these air-fried Greek chickpea patties as a delicious and protein-packed main dish or as a pita filling.
8. Enjoy the crispy exterior and flavorful interior of these chickpea patties.

Per serving: Calories: 250kcal; Fat: 10g; Carbs: 35g; Protein: 10g

132. Crispy Chickpea Polenta Fries with Herbed Yogurt Dip

Preparation time: 15 minutes
Cooking time: 15 minutes
Servings: 4
Ingredients:

- 1 cup polenta, cooked and cooled
- 1 can (15 oz) chickpeas
- 1 tsp. smoked paprika
- 1/2 tsp. garlic powder
- Salt and pepper as required
- Olive oil spray

Herbed Yogurt Dip:

- 1/2 cup Greek yogurt
- 1 tbsp. chopped fresh cilantro
- 1 tbsp. chopped fresh mint
- 1 tbsp. lemon juice
- Salt and pepper as required

Directions:
1. In a food processor, blend cooked polenta until smooth.
2. In a bowl, mix together polenta, chickpeas, smoked paprika, garlic powder, salt, and pepper.
3. Warm up the air fryer to 375 °F.
4. Form the polenta-chickpea mixture into fries and put them in the air fryer basket.
5. Mildly spray fries with olive oil.
6. Air fry for 15 minutes or until the fries are crispy and golden.

For Herbed Yogurt Dip:
1. In your small bowl, combine Greek yogurt, chopped cilantro, chopped mint, lemon juice, salt, and pepper.
2. Serve the crispy chickpea polenta fries with the herbed yogurt dip.

Per serving: Calories: 280kcal; Fat: 5g; Carbs: 48g; Protein: 9g

133. Air-Fried Greek Lemon Herb Quinoa

Preparation time: 10 minutes
Cooking time: 15 minutes
Servings: 4
Ingredients:

- 1 cup quinoa, washed and drained
- 2 cups vegetable broth
- Zest and juice of 1 lemon
- 1 tsp. dried oregano
- 1 tbsp. chopped fresh parsley
- Salt and pepper as required

Directions:
1. Warm up the air fryer to 400 °F.
2. In your bowl, combine quinoa, vegetable broth, lemon zest, lemon juice, dried oregano, chopped parsley, salt, and pepper.
3. Transfer the quinoa mixture to the air fryer basket.
4. Air fry for 15 minutes or 'til the quinoa is cooked and slightly crispy, stirring halfway through.
5. Serve as a side dish or as a base for other Mediterranean dishes.

Per serving: Calories: 180kcal; Fat: 3g; Carbs: 33g; Protein: 6g

134. Lemon Garlic Chickpeas

Preparation time: 10 minutes
Cooking time: 15 minutes
Servings: 4
Ingredients:

- 2 cans (15 oz each) chickpeas
- 2 tbsps. olive oil
- Zest and juice of 1 lemon
- 2 tsps. crushed garlic
- 1 tsp. dried thyme
- Salt and pepper as required

Directions:

1. Warm up the air fryer to 400 °F.
2. In your bowl, toss chickpeas using olive oil, lemon zest, lemon juice, crushed garlic, dried thyme, salt, and pepper.
3. Transfer the chickpea mixture to the air fryer basket.
4. Air fry for 15 minutes or 'til the chickpeas are crispy, shaking the basket occasionally.
5. Serve as a crunchy and zesty snack or as a topping for salads.

Per serving: Calories: 280kcal; Fat: 10g; Carbs: 38g; Protein: 12g

135. Air-Fried Lemon Dill Buckwheat Pancakes

Preparation time: 10 minutes
Cooking time: 10 minutes
Servings: 2
Ingredients:

- 1 cup buckwheat flour
- 1 tbsp. ground flaxseed
- 1 tsp. baking powder
- 1/2 tsp. baking soda
- 1 cup almond milk
- Zest and juice of 1 lemon
- 1 tbsp. chopped fresh dill
- 1 tbsp. maple syrup
- Olive oil spray

Directions:

1. In your bowl, whisk together buckwheat flour, ground flaxseed, baking powder, baking soda, almond milk, lemon zest, lemon juice, chopped dill, and maple syrup.
2. Warm up the air fryer to 375 °F.
3. Mildly spray the air fryer basket using olive oil.
4. Pour pancake batter into the basket to form small pancakes.
5. Air fry for 10 minutes or until the pancakes are cooked through and slightly crispy on the edges.
6. Serve with your favorite toppings.

Per serving: Calories: 280kcal; Fat: 5g; Carbs: 54g; Protein: 7g

136. Air-Fried Falafel Bowl with Brown Rice

Preparation time: 15 minutes
Cooking time: 15 minutes
Servings: 4
Ingredients:

- 1 can (15 oz) chickpeas
- 1/2 cup fresh parsley, chopped
- 1/4 cup red onion, chopped
- 2 pieces garlic, crushed
- 1 tsp. ground cumin
- 1 tsp. ground coriander
- 1/2 tsp. baking powder
- 3 tbsps. chickpea flour
- Salt and pepper as required
- 2 cups cooked brown rice
- 1 cucumber, diced
- 1 cup cherry tomatoes, divided
- 1/4 cup red onion, finely chopped
- 1/4 cup Kalamata olives, cut
- 2 tbsps. hummus (for presenting)

Directions:

1. In the blending container that you have, combine chickpeas, chopped fresh parsley, chopped red onion, crushed garlic, ground cumin, ground coriander, baking powder, chickpea flour, salt, and pepper. Pulse 'til the mixture forms a coarse texture.
2. Form the mixture into falafel balls and put them in to your air fryer basket.
3. Air fry at a temp. of 375 °F for 15 minutes or 'til the falafel is golden and crispy.
4. In serving bowls, assemble cooked brown rice, diced cucumber, divided cherry tomatoes, chopped red onion, and cut Kalamata olives.
5. Top the bowl with air-fried falafel.
6. Serve with a dollop of hummus on the side.
7. Enjoy this air-fried falafel bowl with brown rice as a nutritious and satisfying meal.

Per serving: Calories: 350kcal; Fat: 10g; Carbs: 55g; Protein: 15g

137. Air-Fried Mediterranean Quinoa Patties

Preparation time: 15 minutes
Cooking time: 12 minutes
Servings: 4
Ingredients:

- 1 cup cooked quinoa
- 1 can (15 oz) chickpeas, drained and mashed
- 1/2 cup diced red bell pepper
- 1/4 cup chopped Kalamata olives
- 1/4 cup crumbled feta cheese
- 2 tbsps. chopped fresh parsley
- 1 tsp. ground cumin
- 1 tsp. dried oregano
- Salt and pepper as required
- 1 egg, beaten
- Olive oil spray

Directions:

1. Warm up the air fryer to 375 °F.
2. In your big bowl, combine cooked quinoa, mashed chickpeas, diced red bell pepper, chopped Kalamata olives, crumbled feta, chopped parsley, ground cumin, dried oregano, salt, and pepper.
3. Include beaten egg to the mixture and mix well.
4. Form the mixture into patties and put them in the air fryer basket.
5. Mildly spray the patties with olive oil.
6. Air fry for 12 minutes or until the patties are golden brown and cooked through.

Per serving: Calories: 250kcal; Fat: 10g; Carbs: 32g; Protein: 10g

138. Air-Fried Lemon Herb Quinoa Balls

Preparation time: 15 minutes
Cooking time: 10 minutes
Servings: 4
Ingredients:

- 1 cup cooked quinoa
- 1/4 cup breadcrumbs
- 2 tbsps. grated Parmesan cheese
- 1 tbsp. chopped fresh basil
- 1 tbsp. chopped fresh parsley
- Zest and juice of 1 lemon
- 1 egg, beaten
- Salt and pepper as required
- Olive oil spray

Directions:

1. Warm up the air fryer to 375 °F.
2. In a bowl, combine cooked quinoa, breadcrumbs, Parmesan cheese, chopped basil, chopped parsley, lemon zest, lemon juice, beaten egg, salt, and pepper.
3. Form the mixture into small balls and put them in the air fryer basket.
4. Mildly spray the quinoa balls with olive oil.
5. Air fry for 10 minutes or until the balls are golden brown and cooked through.

Per serving: Calories: 180kcal; Fat: 8g; Carbs: 21g; Protein: 7g

139. Greek-style Lentil Moussaka

Preparation time: 10 minutes
Cooking time: 30 minutes
Servings: 4
Ingredients:

- 1 cup green lentils, cooked
- 1 eggplant, cut into rounds
- 1 zucchini, cut
- 1 onion, finely chopped
- 2 pieces garlic, crushed
- 1 can (14 oz) crushed tomatoes
- 1 tsp. dried oregano
- 1 tsp. ground cinnamon
- Salt and pepper as required
- 2 tbsps. olive oil
- 1 cup Greek yogurt
- 1 egg
- 1/2 cup feta cheese, crumbled
- Fresh parsley, chopped (for garnish)

Directions:

1. Warm up the air fryer to 375 °F.
2. Brush eggplant and zucchini slices using olive oil and air fry for 8-10 minutes or 'til tender.
3. In your skillet, sauté chopped onion and crushed garlic 'til softened.
4. Include cooked green lentils, crushed tomatoes, dried oregano, ground cinnamon, salt, and pepper to the skillet. Simmer for 10 minutes.
5. In your bowl, whisk together Greek yogurt and egg.
6. In your baking dish, layer half of the lentil mixture, followed by a layer of air-fried eggplant and zucchini slices. Repeat the layers.
7. Pour Greek yogurt and egg mixture over the top layer.
8. Crumble feta cheese on top.
9. Bake in to your air fryer for 20 minutes or 'til the top is golden and bubbly.
10. Garnish with chopped fresh parsley prior to presenting.
11. Serve this Greek-style lentil moussaka as a hearty and flavorful dish.
12. Enjoy the layers of lentils, vegetables, and creamy yogurt in each bite.

Per serving: Calories: 400kcal; Fat: 20g; Carbs: 40g; Protein: 15g

140. Lentil and Quinoa Stuffed Zucchini Boats

Preparation time: 10 minutes
Cooking time: 20 minutes
Servings: 4
Ingredients:

- 4 medium zucchini
- 1/2 cup quinoa, uncooked
- 1 cup cooked lentils
- 1/2 cup diced tomatoes
- 1/4 cup diced red onion
- 2 pieces garlic, crushed
- 1 tsp. ground cumin
- 1 tsp. smoked paprika
- Salt and pepper as required
- 1/2 cup crumbled feta cheese
- Olive oil spray

Directions:

1. Warm up the air fryer to 375 °F.
2. Cut each zucchini in half lengthwise then scoop out the flesh, leaving a boat-like structure.
3. In your pot, cook quinoa according to package instructions.
4. In a bowl, combine cooked quinoa, cooked lentils, diced tomatoes, diced red onion, crushed garlic, ground cumin, smoked paprika, salt, and pepper.
5. Stuff each zucchini boat using the quinoa and lentil mixture.
6. Place the stuffed zucchini boats in the air fryer basket.
7. Mildly spray the boats with olive oil.
8. Air fry for 20 minutes or "til the zucchini is tender then the filling is heated through.
9. Sprinkle your crumbled feta over the top prior to presenting.

Per serving: Calories: 250kcal; Fat: 8g; Carbs: 35g; Protein: 12g

 # DESSERTS AND SWEETS

141. Greek-style Almond Cookies (Amygdalota)

Preparation time: 15 minutes
Cooking time: 15 minutes
Servings: 20
Ingredients:

- 2 cups almond flour
- 1/2 cup powdered sugar
- 1/4 cup granulated sugar
- 2 big egg whites
- 1 tsp. almond extract
- 1/2 cup blanched almonds, for topping
- Powdered sugar (for dusting)

Directions:

1. Warm up the air fryer to 325 °F.
2. In your bowl, combine almond flour, powdered sugar, granulated sugar, egg whites, and almond extract. Mix 'til a smooth dough forms.
3. Scoop small portions of the dough and shape them into balls.
4. Put almond balls on a parchment-lined tray then press a blanched almond into the center of each.
5. Air fry for 12-15 minutes or 'til the cookies are mildly golden.
6. Allow the Greek-style almond cookies to cool before dusting with powdered sugar.
7. Enjoy these delightful almond cookies with a tender texture and sweet almond flavor.

Per serving: Calories: 90kcal; Fat: 6g; Carbs: 7g; Protein: 3g

142. Vegan Chocolate Chickpea Brownies

Preparation time: 10 minutes
Cooking time: 20 minutes
Servings: 12
Ingredients:

- 1 can (15 oz) chickpeas
- 1/2 cup almond butter
- 1/3 cup maple syrup
- 1/4 cup cocoa powder
- 1 tsp. vanilla extract
- 1/2 tsp. baking powder
- 1/4 tsp. salt
- Vegan chocolate chips (optional, for topping)

Directions:

1. Warm up the air fryer to 325 °F.
2. In the blending container that you have, blend chickpeas, almond butter, maple syrup, cocoa powder, vanilla extract, baking powder, and salt 'til smooth.
3. Line a baking pan that fits in your air fryer with parchment paper.
4. Disperse brownie batter evenly in the pan.
5. If desired, sprinkle vegan chocolate chips on top.
6. Air fry for 18-20 minutes or 'til the brownies are set.
7. Allow the vegan chocolate chickpea brownies to cool before slicing.
8. Enjoy these fudgy and guilt-free brownies as a satisfying treat.

Per serving: Calories: 150kcal; Fat: 8g; Carbs: 18g; Protein: 4g

143. Mediterranean Orange and Almond Cake

Preparation time: 10 minutes
Cooking time: 25 minutes
Servings: 8
Ingredients:

- 1 cup almond flour
- 1/2 cup all-purpose flour
- 1 tsp. baking powder
- 1/2 tsp. baking soda
- 1/4 tsp. salt
- 1/2 cup unsalted butter, softened
- 1/2 cup sugar
- 2 big eggs
- Zest of 2 oranges
- Juice of 1 orange
- 1/2 tsp. almond extract
- Powdered sugar (for dusting)

Directions:

1. Warm up the air fryer to 325 °F.
2. Grease a cake pan that fits in your air fryer.
3. In your bowl, whisk together almond flour, all-purpose flour, baking powder, baking soda, and salt.
4. In your other bowl, cream together softened butter and sugar 'til light and fluffy.
5. Beat in eggs one at a time, followed by orange zest, orange juice, and almond extract.
6. Gradually place the dry components to the wet components, mixing 'til just combined.
7. Pour batter into the prepared cake pan.
8. Air fry for 20-25 minutes or 'til a toothpick placed into center comes out clean.
9. Let the cake to cool, then dust with powdered sugar prior to presenting.

Per serving: Calories: 300kcal; Fat: 20g; Carbs: 25g; Protein: 6g

144. Lemon Olive Oil Cake with Pistachios

Preparation time: 5 minutes
Cooking time: 25 minutes
Servings: 8
Ingredients:

- 1 cup all-purpose flour
- 1/2 cup almond flour
- 1 tsp. baking powder
- 1/2 tsp. baking soda
- Pinch of salt
- 1/2 cup olive oil
- 3/4 cup sugar
- 2 big eggs
- Zest of 2 lemons
- Juice of 1 lemon
- 1/2 cup plain Greek yogurt
- 1/2 cup shelled pistachios, chopped

Directions:

1. Warm up the air fryer to 325 °F.
2. Grease a cake pan that fits in your air fryer.
3. In your bowl, whisk together baking powder, baking soda, all-purpose flour, almond flour, and a pinch of salt.
4. In your another bowl, beat together olive oil and sugar 'til well combined.
5. Include the eggs one at a time, providing a thorough pounding after every addition.
6. Stir in lemon zest, lemon juice, and Greek yogurt.
7. Gradually place the dry components to the wet components, mixing 'til just combined.
8. Fold in chopped pistachios.
9. Pour batter into the prepared cake pan.
10. Air fry for 25-30 minutes either until a toothpick that has been inserted into the middle comes out clean.
11. Let the lemon olive oil cake to cool prior to presenting.
12. Enjoy a slice of this moist and citrusy cake with a sprinkle of pistachios.

Per serving: Calories: 300kcal; Fat: 18g; Carbs: 30g; Protein: 6g

145. Air-Fried Loukoumades (Honey Puffs)

Preparation time: 15 minutes
Cooking time: 15 minutes
Servings: 20
Ingredients:

- 2 cups all-purpose flour
- 1 packet (2 1/4 tsps.) active dry yeast
- 1 cup warm water
- 1 tbsp. sugar
- 1/2 tsp. salt
- Vegetable oil (for frying)
- Honey (for drizzling)
- Chopped nuts or cinnamon (optional, for garnish)

Directions:

1. In your bowl, dissolve sugar in warm water then add active dry yeast. Allow it to proof for 5-7 minutes.
2. In your big bowl, combine flour and salt. Pour in the yeast mixture and mix 'til a sticky dough forms.
3. Cover the bowl using a kitchen towel then let the dough rise in a warm place for 1-2 hours, or 'til doubled in size.
4. Warm up the air fryer to 375 °F.
5. Scoop small portions of the dough then drop them into the air fryer basket, keeping some distance between each one.
6. Air fry for 10-15 minutes or 'til golden brown then cooked through.
7. Take out the loukoumades from the air fryer and drizzle with honey. Optionally, sprinkle with chopped nuts or cinnamon.
8. Serve these delightful air-fried loukoumades warm.

Per serving: Calories: 150kcal; Fat: 1g; Carbs: 30g; Protein: 3g

146. Air Fryer Greek-style Doughnut Holes

Preparation time: 15 minutes
Cooking time: 10 minutes
Servings: 12
Ingredients:

- 1 cup all-purpose flour
- 1/4 cup sugar
- 1 tsp. baking powder
- 1/4 tsp. baking soda
- 1/4 tsp. ground cinnamon
- Pinch of salt
- 1/2 cup Greek yogurt
- 1 big egg
- 1 tsp. vanilla extract
- 2 tbsps. olive oil
- Powdered sugar (for dusting)

Directions:

1. In your bowl, whisk together all-purpose flour, sugar, baking powder, baking soda, ground cinnamon, and a pinch of salt.
2. In your other bowl, mix Greek yogurt, egg, vanilla extract, and olive oil 'til well combined.
3. Combine the wet and dry components, stirring 'til a sticky dough forms.
4. Warm up the air fryer to 350 °F.
5. Scoop small portions of the dough then roll them into balls.
6. Place doughnut holes in to your air fryer basket, leaving space between each.
7. Air fry for 8-10 minutes or 'til golden brown then cooked through.
8. Allow the doughnut holes to cool slightly before dusting with powdered sugar.
9. Enjoy these delightful Greek-style doughnut holes with a hint of cinnamon.

Per serving: Calories: 90kcal; Fat: 3g; Carbs: 14g; Protein: 2g

147. Baklava Bites

Preparation time: 15 minutes
Cooking time: 15 minutes
Servings: 12
Ingredients:

- 1 cup walnuts, chopped
- 1 cup pistachios, chopped
- 1/2 cup honey
- 1 tsp. ground cinnamon
- 1/2 cup unsalted butter, melted
- 12 sheets phyllo dough

Directions:

1. In your bowl, combine chopped walnuts, chopped pistachios, honey, and ground cinnamon. Mix well.
2. Warm up the air fryer to 350 °F.
3. Lay out one sheet of phyllo dough then brush it lightly with melted butter. Put another sheet on top and repeat 'til you have a stack of three sheets.
4. Cut the phyllo stack into 4 equal squares.
5. Put a spoonful of the nut mixture in the middle of each square.
6. Fold the phyllo squares into triangles, sealing the edges with melted butter.
7. Repeat the process for the remaining phyllo and nut mixture.
8. Place baklava bites in to your air fryer basket.
9. Air fry for 10-15 minutes or 'til golden and crispy.
10. Allow the baklava bites to cool slightly prior to presenting.
11. Enjoy these delightful baklava bites with a crunchy exterior and sweet, nutty filling.

Per serving: Calories: 200kcal; Fat: 15g; Carbs: 15g; Protein: 4g

148. Almond and Orange Biscotti

Preparation time: 15 minutes
Cooking time: 15 minutes
Servings: 16
Ingredients:

- 2 cups all-purpose flour
- 1 cup almonds, chopped
- 1/2 cup sugar
- 1 tsp. baking powder
- 1/4 tsp. salt
- Zest of 2 oranges
- 2 big eggs
- 1 tsp. almond extract
- 1/2 tsp. vanilla extract

Directions:

1. Warm up the air fryer to 325 °F.
2. In your bowl, whisk together all-purpose flour, chopped almonds, sugar, baking powder, salt, and orange zest.
3. In your other bowl, beat eggs, almond extract, and vanilla extract 'til well combined.
4. Gradually place the dry components to the wet components, mixing 'til a dough forms.
5. Split the dough in half and shape each portion into a log.
6. Place logs on a parchment-lined tray that fits in your air fryer.
7. Air fry for 12-15 minutes or 'til the biscotti logs are golden and firm to the touch.
8. Allow the logs to cool for a few minutes before slicing them into biscotti.
9. Enjoy these Almond and Orange Biscotti with a cup of coffee or tea.

Per serving: Calories: 140kcal; Fat: 6g; Carbs: 18g; Protein: 4g

149. Orange Blossom Water Rice Pudding

Preparation time: 5 minutes
Cooking time: 25 minutes
Servings: 4
Ingredients:

- 1/2 cup Arborio rice
- 2 cups whole milk
- 1/4 cup sugar
- 1/2 tsp. vanilla extract
- 1/4 tsp. orange blossom water
- Orange zest (for garnish)

Directions:

1. In to your air fryer basket, combine Arborio rice, whole milk, and sugar.
2. Air fry at a temp. of 325 °F for 20-25 minutes, mixing irregularly, 'til the rice is cooked and the mixture thickens.
3. Stir in your vanilla extract and orange blossom water.
4. Let the rice pudding to cool prior to presenting.
5. Garnish with orange zest for a refreshing touch.
6. Enjoy the aromatic and creamy Orange Blossom Water Rice Pudding.

Per serving: Calories: 200kcal; Fat: 5g; Carbs: 30g; Protein: 6g

150. Air Fryer Fig and Walnut Stuffed Phyllo Pastry

Preparation time: 15 minutes
Cooking time: 10 minutes
Servings: 8
Ingredients:

- 1/2 cup dried figs, chopped
- 1/4 cup walnuts, chopped
- 1 tbsp. honey
- 1/2 tsp. cinnamon
- 8 sheets phyllo dough
- 1/4 cup melted butter

Directions:

1. Warm up the air fryer to 375 °F.
2. In your bowl, mix chopped dried figs, chopped walnuts, honey, and cinnamon.
3. Lay out one sheet of your phyllo dough, brush it lightly with melted butter, and place another sheet on top. Repeat 'til you have four layers.
4. Spoon the fig and walnut mixture along one edge of the phyllo stack.
5. Roll the phyllo tightly around the filling to form a log.
6. Repeat the process for the remaining sheets of phyllo and filling.
7. Place stuffed phyllo pastries in to your air fryer basket.
8. Air fry for 8-10 minutes or 'til golden brown and crispy.
9. Allow the pastries to cool slightly before slicing.
10. Enjoy these delightful Air Fryer Fig and Walnut Stuffed Phyllo Pastries with a perfect balance of sweetness and crunch.

Per serving: Calories: 180kcal; Fat: 8g; Carbs: 25g; Protein: 4g

Conclusion

As we near the end of this culinary journey together, I want to share something more personal, a snippet of my life. Behind every recipe and every tip on making the most of your air fryer, there's a story, there's my heart. Creating this book was not just a professional journey but an emotional voyage filled with challenges and triumphs, moments spent in the kitchen among trials, successes, and the inevitable mishap. Every page reflects not just my passion for cooking but also my deep desire to share something truly special with you.

I also want to remind you how precious your support is to me. Every thought you share about this book, every reflection, is like a beacon guiding my path as an author. Your words not only help me grow and improve but also light the way for other readers, helping them discover the magic of Mediterranean cooking through the air fryer.

I understand that behind every review is a person, with their experiences and expectations, and I assure you that I will read each of your impressions with attention and gratitude, welcoming every suggestion and critique as a precious gift. It's this exchange, this connection between us, that makes the world of books so extraordinary.

To make all this even more personal, I'd like you to imagine me, in my kitchen, surrounded by the ingredients I've talked about, hands deep in dough, smiling and content to share my passion with you. This image, though I can't physically show it to you, embodies the essence of what I've tried to convey: love for a simple, healthy, and flavorful cuisine. It's in these moments of creation and sharing that the true spirit of this book lies.

If you feel that the pages you've explored and the flavors you've discovered have enriched your table and spirit, I invite you to scan the QR code for those who wish to share this journey with me. Your voice has immense power, and every word you choose to share about this book helps build a bridge between us, a bond made of culinary experiences, learning, and shared growth.

I thank you from the bottom of my heart for being part of this journey, for every moment you've decided to spend discovering the pages I've written for you.

With affection and a pinch of sea salt,
Olivia Grace Thompson

30 Days Meal Plan

Day	Breakfast	Lunch	Dinner	Dessert
1	Air-fried shakshuka bites	Mediterranean Quinoa Salad with Roasted Vegetables	Mediterranean Baked Haddock with Olives	Baklava Bites
2	Herbed feta and tomato breakfast quesadillas	Eggplant and Chickpea Stew	Air-fried Crab Cakes with Remoulade Sauce	Air-Fried Loukoumades (Honey Puffs)
3	Lemon and herb ricotta stuffed mushrooms	Air Fryer Lamb Kofta Skewers	Stuffed Grape Leaves (Dolma) with Rice and Herbs	Mediterranean Orange and Almond Cake
4	Air-fried olive and herb breadsticks	Lemon Rosemary Air-Fried Turkey Breast	Air-Fried Walnut and Date Stuffed Figs	Air Fryer Greek-Style Doughnut Holes
5	Mediterranean breakfast pita pockets	Roasted Red Pepper and Feta Stuffed Squid	Mediterranean Beef Kebabs with Tomato and Onion	Lemon Olive Oil Cake with Pistachios
6	Greek-style air fryer bagel with cream cheese	Spicy Harissa Grilled Prawns	Garlic and Herb Marinated Air Fryer Chicken Breasts	Greek-Style Almond Cookies (Amygdalota)
7	Spinach and feta breakfast wraps	Vegan Moussaka	Vegan Spinach and Artichoke Dip	Vegan Chocolate Chickpea Brownies
8	Air fryer greek omelet roll-ups	Ratatouille Stuffed Zucchini Boats	Greek Lemon Garlic Roasted Potatoes	Orange Blossom Water Rice Pudding
9	Tomato and olive bruschetta toast	Air-Fried Honey Mustard Glazed Chicken Drumettes	Lemon Oregano Grilled Chicken Skewers	Air Fryer Fig and Walnut Stuffed Phyllo Pastry
10	Mediterranean veggie breakfast skewers	Italian Herb Crusted Pork Tenderloin	Mediterranean Lamb and Chickpea Stew	Almond and Orange Biscotti
11	Greek-style air fryer breakfast potatoes	Mediterranean Baked Cod with Cherry Tomatoes	Baked Lemon Garlic Herb Salmon Pockets	Baklava Bites
12	Lemon and herb ricotta stuffed mushrooms	Air Fryer Salmon with Dill and Lemon	Shrimp and Spinach Stuffed Squid Tubes	Air-Fried Loukoumades (Honey Puffs)
13	Air-fried mediterranean quiche bites	Vegan Spanakopita with Dairy-Free Feta	Air Fryer Sweet Potato and Chickpea Buddha Bowl	Mediterranean Orange and Almond Cake
14	Tomato and olive breakfast flatbreads	Air-Fried Falafel Wrap with Tahini Sauce	Mediterranean Quinoa-Stuffed Bell Peppers	Air Fryer Greek-Style Doughnut Holes
15	Air-fried olive and herb breadsticks	Mediterranean Lamb Chops with Mint Chimichurri	Crispy Italian Herb Pork Chops	Lemon Olive Oil Cake with Pistachios
16	Greek-style air fryer bagel with cream cheese	Harissa Marinated Grilled Chicken Thighs	Greek-Style Stuffed Cabbage Rolls with Ground Beef	Greek-Style Almond Cookies (Amygdalota)

17	Mediterranean breakfast pita pockets	Air-Fried Honey Sesame Cinnamon Pita Chips	Vegan Eggplant Caponata with Crispy Pita	Vegan Chocolate Chickpea Brownies
18	Spinach and feta breakfast wraps	Mediterranean Roasted Vegetable Platter	Air-Fried Greek Zucchini Fritters	Orange Blossom Water Rice Pudding
19	Lemon and herb ricotta stuffed mushrooms	Lemon Garlic Herb Air-Fried Shrimp	Garlic and Herb Grilled Clams	Air Fryer Fig and Walnut Stuffed Phyllo Pastry
20	Air fryer greek omelet roll-ups	Grilled Swordfish Steaks with Olive Tapenade	Air-Fried Fish and Chips with Greek Yogurt Tartar Sauce	Baklava Bites
21	Tomato and olive bruschetta toast	Greek-Style Stuffed Peppers with Rice and Vegetables	Vegan Mediterranean Cauliflower Steaks	Air-Fried Loukoumades (Honey Puffs)
22	Mediterranean veggie breakfast skewers	Air-Fried Mediterranean Scallops	Spinach and Olive Vegan Stuffed Mushrooms	Lemon Olive Oil Cake with Pistachios
23	Greek-style air fryer breakfast potatoes	Herb-Crusted Air Fryer Tilapia	Grilled Sardines with Lemon and Oregano	Almond and Orange Biscotti
24	Lemon and herb ricotta stuffed mushrooms	Baked Italian Herb Turkey Meatballs	Greek Lemon Butter Shrimp Skewers	Air Fryer Greek-Style Doughnut Holes
25	Air-fried mediterranean quiche bites	Greek-Style Chicken Pita Wraps with Tahini Sauce	Moroccan-Spiced Lamb Burgers	Mediterranean Orange and Almond Cake
26	Tomato and olive breakfast flatbreads	Grilled Swordfish Steaks with Olive Tapenade	Air-Fried Cajun Chicken Thighs	Baklava Bites
27	Air-fried olive and herb breadsticks	Air-Fried Coconut Shrimp with Mango Salsa	Air-Fried Greek Zucchini Fritters	Air Fryer Fig and Walnut Stuffed Phyllo Pastry
28	Mediterranean breakfast pita pockets	Mediterranean Stuffed Mussels with Herbs	Garlic and Herb Grilled Clams	Greek-Style Almond Cookies (Amygdalota)
29	Spinach and feta breakfast wraps	Greek Lamb Burger with Tzatziki Sauce	Air-Fried Fish and Chips with Greek Yogurt Tartar Sauce	Orange Blossom Water Rice Pudding
30	Air fryer greek omelet roll-ups	Balsamic Glazed Air Fryer Chicken Quarters	Greek-Style Shrimp and Feta Orzo	Vegan Chocolate Chickpea Brownies

Conversion Chart

Volume Equivalents (Liquid)

US Standard	US Standard (oz.)	Metric (approximate)
2 tbsps.	1 fl. oz.	30 milliliter
¼ cup	2 fl. oz.	60 milliliter
½ cup	4 fl. oz.	120 milliliter
1 cup	8 fl. oz.	240 milliliter
1½ cups	12 fl. oz.	355 milliliter
2 cups or 1 pint	16 fl. oz.	475 milliliter
4 cups or 1 quart	32 fl. oz.	1 Liter
1 gallon	128 fl. oz.	4 Liter

Volume Equivalents (Dry)

US Standard	Metric (approximate)
⅛ tsp.	0.5 milliliter
¼ tsp.	1 milliliter
½ tsp.	2 milliliter
¾ tsp.	4 milliliter
1 tsp.	5 milliliter
1 tbsp.	15 milliliter
¼ cup	59 milliliter
⅓ cup	79 milliliter
½ cup	118 milliliter
⅔ cup	156 milliliter
¾ cup	177 milliliter
1 cup	235 milliliter
2 cups or 1 pint	475 milliliter
3 cups	700 milliliter
4 cups or 1 quart	1 Liter

Oven Temperatures

Fahrenheit (F)	Celsius (C) (approximate)
250 °F	120 °C
300 °F	150 °C
325 °F	165 °C
350 °F	180 °C
375 °F	190 °C
400 °F	200 °C
425 °F	220 °C
450 °F	230 °C

Weight Equivalents

US Standard	Metric (approximate)
1 tbsp.	15 g
½ oz.	15 g
1 oz.	30 g
2 oz.	60 g
4 oz.	115 g
8 oz.	225 g
12 oz.	340 g
16 oz. or 1 lb.	455 g

Index

Greek-style Stuffed Cabbage Rolls with Ground Beef; 62

Greek-style Stuffed Peppers with Rice and Vegetables; 36

Grilled Asparagus with Lemon and Parmesan; 73

Grilled Halloumi and Watermelon Salad; 67

Grilled Sardines with Lemon and Oregano; 48

Grilled Swordfish Steaks with Olive Tapenade; 46

Harissa Marinated Grilled Chicken Thighs; 55

Herb-Crusted Air Fryer Tilapia; 48

Herbed Feta and Tomato Breakfast Quesadillas; 18

Hummus-Stuffed Mini Bell Peppers; 27

Italian Herb Crusted Pork Tenderloin; 53

Lemon and Herb Ricotta Stuffed Mushrooms; 15

Lemon and Olive Oil Roasted Potatoes; 63

Lemon Garlic Chickpeas; 83

Lemon Garlic Herb Air-Fried Shrimp; 45

Lemon Garlic Marinated Olives; 26

Lemon Garlic Roasted Brussels Sprouts; 66

Lemon Herb Air-Fried Sorghum Salad; 69

Lemon Olive Oil Cake with Pistachios; 90

Lemon Oregano Grilled Chicken Skewers; 60

Lemon Rosemary Air-Fried Turkey Breast; 54

Lentil and Quinoa Stuffed Zucchini Boats; 87

Lentil and Vegetable Stuffed Grape Leaves (Dolma); 77

Mediterranean Baked Cod with Cherry Tomatoes; 51

Mediterranean Baked Haddock with Olives; 43

Mediterranean Beef Kebabs with Tomato and Onion; 55

Mediterranean Breakfast Burritos with Hummus; 13

Mediterranean Breakfast Pita Pockets; 21

Mediterranean Bruschetta with Tomato and Basil; 24

Mediterranean Couscous with Roasted Vegetables; 76

Mediterranean Lamb and Chickpea Stew; 56

Mediterranean Lamb Chops with Mint Chimichurri; 59

Mediterranean Orange and Almond Cake; 90

Mediterranean Quinoa Salad with Roasted Vegetables; 38

Mediterranean Quinoa-stuffed Bell Peppers; 41

Mediterranean Roasted Vegetable Platter; 36

Mediterranean Stuffed Grape Leaves (Dolma); 30

Mediterranean Stuffed Mussels with Herbs; 51

Mediterranean Veggie Breakfast Skewers; 22

Mediterranean Veggie Omelet; 16

Moroccan-spiced Lamb Burgers; 58

Mushroom and Spinach Air Fryer Risotto; 78

Olive and Herb Pita Chips; 29

Orange Blossom Water Rice Pudding; 93

Quinoa and Chickpea Stuffed Bell Peppers; 81

Ratatouille Stuffed Zucchini Boats; 37

Roasted Eggplant and Tomato Caprese Salad; 63

Roasted Red Pepper and Feta Egg Cups; 17

Roasted Red Pepper and Feta Stuffed Squid; 45

Roasted Red Pepper and Walnut Dip; 27

Shrimp and Spinach Stuffed Squid Tubes; 52

Spicy Harissa Grilled Prawns; 49

Spinach and Artichoke Dip Stuffed Mushrooms; 23

Spinach and Artichoke Stuffed Portobello Mushrooms; 33

Spinach and Feta Breakfast Wraps; 18

Spinach and Feta Stuffed Breakfast Peppers; 21

Spinach and Olive Vegan Stuffed Mushrooms; 41

Stuffed Grape Leaves (Dolma) with Rice and Herbs; 38

Sundried Tomato and Olive Frittata Muffins; 15

Tomato and Basil Bruschetta Cups; 32

Tomato and Olive Breakfast Flatbreads; 14

Tomato and Olive Bruschetta Toast; 20

Vegan Chocolate Chickpea Brownies; 89

Vegan Eggplant Caponata with Crispy Pita; 39

Vegan Mediterranean Cauliflower Steaks; 42

Vegan Moussaka; 34

Vegan Spanakopita with Dairy-Free Feta; 35

Vegan Spinach and Artichoke Dip; 39

Zucchini and Feta Fritters; 29

Made in United States
Orlando, FL
26 November 2024